The Art of Motivational Listening

Creative Ideas for Effective Leaders

Other Works by Adam G. Fleming

Fiction
White Buffalo Gold, ©2012.
Autographed copies available.
Available on Amazon or get an autographed copy at
www.whitebuffalogold.wordpress.com/purchase.

Theater
A Pebble among the Rocks, ©2010.
*This play is ideal for community theater productions. The cast of
10-12 includes multiple roles for senior citizens. Please contact the
author at adam.fleming.lifecoach@gmail.com for a free pdf and to
discuss royalty options.*

Screenplay
White Buffalo Gold (working title), ©2015.
By Adam G. Fleming and Michelle Oyer
*We are seeking a producer or major sponsor for independent pro-
duction at the time of this printing. Contact author.*

The Art of Motivational Listening

Creative Ideas for Effective Leaders

Adam G. Fleming

Foreword
Mark Whitacre, Ph.D.

Entrust Source Publishers
Rio Rico, AZ

Entrust Source Publishers

For more information, please go to: www.entrustsource.com.

ISBN-10: 1942308086
ISBN-13: 978-1-942308-08-9

Printed in the United States of America

Cover created by Entrust Source LLC, Judy Buckert

Back cover photograph by Bryan Chris Photography

All photographs (other than in the appendix or otherwise noted) courtesy of the author

Photographs in appendix provided by respective persons

Entrust Source Publishers
281 Camino la Pasida
Rio Rico, AZ 85648
www.entrustsourcepublishers.com

For Megan, my love, who keeps throwing me knuckleballs.

For Timothy, Jonathan, Benjamin and Acadia: I really want to hear what you have to say. Remind me often.

Contents

Foreword

The Right Man

Adam Fleming is just the right man to write this book. In this book, Adam provides an extraordinary glimpse into the world of motivational listening. Almost everyone wants to become a much better listener. But, how do we get there? How do we improve?

I first met Adam a few years ago in Indianapolis where he was my instructor in a Leadership Coaching Training (Level 1). I was so impressed with him, and the training was life-changing for me! Therefore, a few months later, I traveled back to Indianapolis in order to enroll in his Intensive Leadership Coaching Training (Level 2). By then, I was hooked!

Leadership Coaching taught me how to be a much better listener and how to ask powerful questions. Even my wife said, "Thank God for this training because you have never listened this well in over three decades prior to this class." It made me a better husband, a better father and a better leader. Thank God for Adam Fleming and his training. I highly recommend all the readers of this book to take that training. It will change your life. There is no substitute for this training.

After learning better listening skills from Adam that impacted my life, I was excited to read his new book prior to publication. Adam is a deep thinker, and he is a visionary. You will clearly see that trait as you read this exceptional book. He wants everyone to become better listeners and he spends most waking hours of his life trying to help others get there. Adam is certainly a servant leader.

This book is not a training course, nor is it meant to be. However, Adam's book is an excellent resource and supplement for anyone wanting to become a better listener. I highly recommend for you to read this book along with some training. It will stimulate your thinking process about the art of motivational listening. It is a MUST read!

Mark E. Whitacre, Ph.D.
National Director of Field Ministry & Support for CBMC

Dr. Mark Whitacre is an Ivy League Ph.D. and is considered the highest-ranked executive of any Fortune 500 company to become a whistleblower in U.S. history. He was responsible for uncovering the ADM price-fixing scandal in the early 1990s. His undercover work with the FBI during the ADM scandal was the inspiration for the 2009 major motion picture, "The Informant," starring Matt Damon as Mark Whitacre, and the 2010 Discovery Channel documentary "Undercover."

Introduction

What's a motivational *listener?*

Executives and lead pastors alike know there are limitations regarding how long anyone will remember anything from a motivational speech or sermon. After six weeks, your retention without follow up is around 1 percent. Yet even in today's age, corporations continue to put speakers in their budget every year, sometimes to the tune of tens of thousands of dollars. Churches and non-profits do it too; they bring in an itinerant preacher and everyone gets psyched up. Plenty of people are aware that retention is increased dramatically with follow-up coaching. Of course, you have to speak occasionally to motivate people, but the hard part is budgeting time and space for listening.

I used to have *motivational speaker* on my business card, but on principle, I won't do it anymore: I won't take speaking engagements that don't include a follow-up package—at least with the organization's leader, if not with key team members. Which is more important, the speech itself, or great follow-up? When we want to get motivated, we hope someone can help. We need more than a great speaker. We need a motivational listener who will work with us over the long haul. Lots of people want to become better listeners. Tons of authors and leadership gurus talk about it. I'm convinced there's only one way to get there: take a training course.

This book is not a training course, nor is it even remotely a decent substitute. It is not, as far as I'm concerned, even a potential textbook for a training. This book is more like a dietary supplement for listeners, something to add to the exercise and healthy eating routines of training programs. It's a series of essays designed to prod you to think differently, mostly about listening. There is no diet pill that works without the critical sacrifice of training exercises and healthy eating. Learning to listen is no different.

What follows is a compilation of essays designed for your own reflection and meditation on your artistic style as a motivational listener. It is not a how-to book. The science of listening can be studied as a skill set and there are some great how-to books available.

This is the process to becoming an artist of any kind. An artful listener and motivator is no different: artists are initially inspired by style (when their own style is quite raw), then they must work to master method, and finally, they develop a style on the other side. So this book is for those who want to be inspired by style, and those who are crafting a style. You may be inspired by the works of Monet. A painting instructor can teach you the methodology to use a Color Wheel—red and blue make purple— and even create combinations of three or more colors that are considered aesthetically pleasing, and a coach trainer can teach someone to use the GROW model, SMART goals, or the Wheel of Life, the mechanics of a session where you listen fully, but you can't teach style. This book is intended to prompt you to think about and discover your own style of listening and motivating, and I hope to approach it in the same way any art is taught or discussed: in metaphor, simile, stories, and other forms of analogy. I have chosen to write about my profession as regards the artfulness of it rather than address the scientific aspects, because

I am well aware that other writers have given you the coaching color-wheel methodology with a great deal of excellence. Consider this book a companion volume to your other coaching and motivation books—meditations on style to go with the scientific method you'll learn elsewhere.

This book is for you if you are curious about people. You do not need to be a professional listener, earning your living as a coach or coach trainer, pastor, counselor, spiritual director, consultant, social worker or other listening profession. You just have to be curious about people.

Some of you have read some of the how-to books and have taken some training in coaching methodology or another listening profession. You have some level of expertise in a listening profession or vocation, so my hope for you is that this book helps you think about and continue to hone your own unique style as you grow.

Others of you have only read about the methodology of coaching but haven't gotten training, still others haven't read or studied anything in this genre until now. To both of you, I hope that this book inspires you, and I unequivocally suggest that your next move is to take some training. After all, it is the style of a musician that makes one want to learn guitar when one is small. We don't see the hours practicing scales, but we must be inspired first by someone's style. My friends who are self-taught guitarists eventually find that without classes they have knowledge gaps. The same goes for listening and motivating.

Get a new notebook or open a new doc or folder in your computer. Think through the questions which you'll find at the end of most of the essays, and jot down a few responses. Write down stuff you disagree with, and email me (adam.fleming. lifecoach@gmail.com) or comment on my blog (www.adam

gfleming.com) after you've read the book. Who knows, your comments could influence my next series of articles!

There are a variety of terms I've introduced through the course of this book. I organized the essays in such a fashion so that if you read it from the front cover to the back, you will get the definition of a term in the earliest essay in which it appears. However, if you'd like to jump about and read pieces as they grab your interest, but you come across a term that's foreign, just refer to the glossary at the back. The glossary will cross reference the first essay in which the term is introduced, so you can find it.

This book primarily contains glimpses into my own philosophy of listening, as well as some bits on leadership; culture; motivation; empathy and reading; art; truth, goodness and greatness; et cetera. As far as using this book to improve your listening skills, I have one primary suggestion: use it to generate conversations. Talk to your friends and colleagues about an idea that's challenging you, or correspond with me. My hope for you is that if you've already had some training, you'll want more; or at the very least, listening will be something you meditate on more often. If you haven't gotten training, I hope you'll be inspired to get some. You don't have to be on a changing career track to benefit from training to become a better listener.

If you were giving yourself a motivational speech, what would you say? What would it mean to you to have someone really listen to that and believe that it could happen?

Adam Fleming

You can look like you're listening when you're not—
but your response will betray you.

Article 1

Oklahoma, OK!

W hen I was five years old, my parents took me to the high school gym to see a production of the musical *Oklahoma*. At the end of the performance, I told my mother, "Mom: when I grow up, I want to be on stage!"

What was it that appealed to me? The hours of rehearsal? The voice lessons? The late nights those students put in with homework afterward and the lack of financial incentive for their work? The crucible of becoming a team, conflicts with the director or co-actors who aren't learning their lines fast enough or showing up on time or taking rehearsal seriously? Certainly not.

Initially, we are attracted to a particular form of art because of someone's personal style. Perhaps it was the swagger and confidence of the main characters. Perhaps it was the rich harmonies of the chorus line. Maybe it was the romanticism of the lead character getting the girl (I knew my parents were in love; the power and significance of romance was not lost on my five-year-old self). Maybe it was the six guns, cowboy boots and bandannas, the glamour of costumes and the set. Maybe it was the opportunity to pretend to be someone else; the fantasy and escape. And maybe it was the applause at the end; the power to move people. Probably it was the combination of all these things so that the phrase "being on stage" indicated a lifestyle that appealed to me.

From 1997–1999, as an outreach, I ran a punk/hardcore/ alternative music club in the basement of our church's building. We booked national Gospel Rock acts such as Brandtson, Zao, Ghoti Hook, Starflier 59, Embodyment, Buck, The Channelsurfers, and Ballydowse. We allowed local bands to play, too—high school kids who wanted to "be on stage," as five-year-old me would have said. Most of the high school kids who attended shows there would tell you they loved "all kinds of music" and then go on to tell you the exceptions, which usually included classical, rap and country western—some pretty broad swaths of the musical landscape. Their passion for music was usually driven by a certain narrowly-defined style ("It's sort of a poppy, post-core sound, more melodic, like emo" or "straightedge ONLY" or "I mostly like ska, stuff you can actually dance to") and whatever their thing was, they wouldn't be caught dead with anything else in their collection.

Those who are still involved with music today eventually expanded well beyond the scope of hard rock and may even be bluegrass or folk performers now. Their style morphed as they examined the rich tapestry of possibilities beyond their initial attraction to the style of a certain band when they were 15.

Similarly, we who are interested in listening are influenced and inspired by the style of a particular person and then we need to branch out and get influences from many others. Gary Horst was my first life coach (when I didn't know any famous coaches other than in the sports world). Rich Foss was one of my earliest influences in writing (though I was aware of many famous authors, however, it was a not-famous man I knew personally that showed me you don't have to be famous to write really good fiction). I wouldn't be the coach and writer I am today without having interacted with dozens of other coaches and writers. Those who inspire us are also allowed to influence us.

The direction I've taken may not match up with what I thought I would be after watching *Oklahoma* at age five, but I still find ways to scratch my itch for "being on stage" with public speaking and leading coach training seminars. I've also gotten involved at various times with community theater; somewhere along the line, I recognized that the aspects of our identity are sometimes vocational and at other times fit better in the semi-wild hedgerows of our lives (places of stillness and exploration where any productivity is haphazard—more on hedgerows later).

❖ Who is the best listener you know? What makes them so good at it? Who motivates you?

❖ Who arouses your curiosity? Whose story would you like to hear?

❖ Where are your knowledge and skill gaps as a listener? What sort of additional training would be valuable?

Article 2

Brevity

Silence is Golden. Duct Tape is Silver.
—Tee Shirt Slogan

When you are a public speaker, keep it short and stick to three main points. Leave space for thought. This is called a pause. Most speakers don't realize how essential a pause is for their listeners!

(I have failed at this. Audience reaction was tepid.)

When you are supposed to be listening, and you take a moment to talk, keep it even shorter. Stick to the illustration of only one principle. Then ask another open-ended question.

When you are writing about listening, remember that now you are a public speaker, on paper. Leave space for thought. Don't answer all your own questions.

❖ Then return to a listening posture.

Article 3

Fermata

Oftentimes when we're really trying hard to ask a great question that will open up miles of possibilities, we take a stab at it when there's a three-second pause. We're so eager! But leaving the pause intact can be a lot like observing the "rest" or fermata in music. If you don't endure the suspense, you kill the moment. But if you can en-dure....

Figure 1. Fermata.

The best stuff someone has to say comes after you've avoided finishing their sentence, avoided putting a question mark in the middle of their fermata, after you've waited what seems an eternity but is probably only 30 seconds—that's six or seven breaths for most of us—and the gold mine appears. Whatever it is (that really important thing) that someone is *trying to say* is said *after the pause.*

If you want to try it, next time someone is having trouble finishing their phrase, try exhaling regularly six times. Don't rush like a sixth-grade snare drum player.

❖ Next time you're listening to someone and they pause in their speaking, listen to yourself breathe and imagine rest-ing for a bar, or four, or eight bars of music.

Article 4

The knuckleball

What is a listening posture? We know that it refers to a mental or spiritual attitude, but what is it like: Standing, sitting, lying prone?

A baseball catcher spends his career in a squatting position or crouch; an awkward position that ruins knees and sometimes shortens careers. Many of the greatest coaches were former catchers because of the unique way their role on the field prepares them for the coaching job: catchers are often said to be the on-field coach.

The catcher has several jobs. The first is to call for a pitch so they set things in motion. (This is similar to a listener asking a powerful coaching question.)

The second is to catch the pitch. (Hear the answer—gather it in.)

If the catcher fails to catch the pitch on the baseball field, it can mean disaster. So the alternative is to knock the ball down to the ground. It's not ideal, but it can keep a runner from scoring. If the catcher misses the ball and a runner scores, the team may even lose the game. Ironically, the pitcher is the one who is said to have "won" or "lost" the game. But much credit is often due this on-field coach: sometimes they call a good game. Sometimes they catch cleanly and throw a runner out. And sometimes, they just knock the ball down, and that's good enough.

The hardest pitch to catch is the knuckleball. This throw involves putting no spin on the ball so that the ambient air may direct the ball: herky-jerky, down, wiggly-wiggles, or even, in defiance of gravity, up! It can be nearly impossible to hit, but is also very difficult to catch, because the catcher can't anticipate its direction; it doesn't go fast, and it doesn't go straight.

The pitcher can't spend his time worrying about whether or not the ball will be caught. A knuckleballer puts a great deal of concentration into the pitch: it is a difficult art to throw a round ball without putting any spin on it. It can be impossible to hit, yes, but when thrown incorrectly, it can also be the easiest pitch for a batter to hit. His job in that moment is only to execute the pitch.

A really good listener is always calling for the knuckleball. The listener says, "Give me something without any spin, something I can't anticipate, and I'll knock it down and help you turn it into a win."

❖ When was the last time someone surprised you with their thoughts? How did it feel to be entrusted with their knuckleball?

Article 5

You're a candidate for a wax job

W hen I was 39 years old, Haley, my barber—no, I should say, *my stylist*, tried an up-sell on me. "I have other customers who are men around your age," she said, "and, well, a lot of them have me wax their nose hair and eyebrows. And ... well, you know ... you're a candidate."

When I got done laughing about her skillful—even political—use of words to inform me that my nostrils and unibrow were less than sophisticated, I relented and allowed her to place piping hot firebrands covered in molten wax up my nose. I even agreed to pay extra for this. And, you know, the pain isn't really that bad. But the hair keeps growing. It seems I'm a candidate for life.

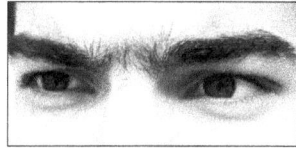

Figure 2. Not the author's actual eyebrows.

Not long ago, my wife, Megan, and I had a gut-level conversation with our friend, Jonathan. Jonathan's not trained specifically as a life coach, but we've been meeting with him for oversight (because coaching is my milieu) and I had been thinking about him critically in his capacity. Since we all value honesty, I admitted to him that I was a little dissatisfied when seeing him through that coaching lens. So we talked about what it is exactly that he does, how it differs from coaching, this oversight thing, and finally Megan and I decided upon the term "oracle" (which made him delightfully uncomfortable. I

11

mean, it gave him the creepy-crawlies. He did this little freaked-out boogie dance. It's going to become a classic story, larger than life. Already is.).

In the course of this conversation, he reminded me of something I've known all along: I'm really nice about it, but I'm bull-headed and though my marriage is good, I still need someone who has permission to call me out and help me stay on track even when the marriage isn't my top priority for growth! (Guess what, our marriage isn't always the top priority. Build a great foundation, and you can focus on other things.) In other words, even though I'm pretty happy with a lot of things right now, *I'm a candidate* for the oracle. In fact, I'm a candidate for life. The marriage, like eyebrows, needs consistent grooming.

I may not say a whole lot more about character throughout the rest of the book. For one thing, just about every other book on leadership and listening has already addressed character. I'll just assume you know it's important—important enough that you are already giving attention to the area of character growth in your life.

If you want a life of growth and you know that the nose hairs of character have to be cleared away like brush in dry season before a fire breaks out, then you're always going to be a candidate. You need to be listened to so that you do great listening. So get a coach. Or a prophetic oracle. Or a pastor who's not a puppet for what the congregation wants—someone to whom you are willing to abdicate your considerable power of independence (I'm assuming you're reading this from a Western perspective).

You may or may not pay this person for their role in your life, but you want to develop relationships you won't voluntarily terminate. Ideally you'll have multiple people who can call you out. Maybe it's a mentor who expects you to exceed their own success and who will challenge you when they see you getting slacker-y or bull-headed, who pushes you, even on the stuff you're really good at—your marriage, or your business ethics. Find someone you trust, and let them wax whenever you wane.

❖ So you want to provide accountability. Where do you need life-long accountability, and how will you get it?

Article 6

Developing a philosophy of listening

History is merely a list of surprises.
It can only prepare us to be surprised yet again.[1]
—Kurt Vonnegut

O ne day in 2010, I was volunteering at our local soup kitchen when I walked past a bookshelf full of romance novels and in a moment of serendipity, *The Black Swan: The Impact of the Highly Improbable* said, "Read me." Even the way the spine is designed says, "This is not a romance novel." This is probably why it jumped off the shelf at me—the different spine. People do judge books by their covers, or even more rapidly, by their spines. I'm aware of books. I notice when they're around similar to when a teenage boy notices girls. OK, maybe I don't notice books quite that intently. But anyway, I seized the day, asked *The Black Swan* out for a date (borrowed the book permanently), and began to read … serious philosophy. Maybe for the first time in 15 years.

In fact, I had read *Why Art Cannot Be Taught* by James Elkins a few years before but perhaps didn't see it as the philosophical book that it is. Once I read *The Black Swan,* I had to admit to myself I was reading stuff that was a bit over my head which was good. "Maybe," I thought, "it's a book I will need to read twice." From there, I read *Zen and the Art of Motorcycle*

Maintenance, and so on. I began to engage philosophy in a much more serious way than I had during my undergrad years. This year (2015), I encountered my former philosophy professor at an arts conference and we had lunch. I apologized for my lack of interest and intellectual rigor in her Intro to Philosophy class so many years ago. She just smiled and hugged me. I realized here was someone I hadn't appreciated properly at all. I had been missing out on this friendship with Dr. Jo-Ann Brant, and it was all my fault. I had taken out my disinterest in philosophy at the time on her. What a jerk I can be. But she simply forgave the former me and seemed glad to hear about what I was doing.

My attitude in college had been the same attitude General Custer had at West Point who finished last in his class for his poor performance in Draftsmanship. Custer didn't care about learning to draw and he nearly flunked out of West Point. Drawing, for a military officer in the 1800s, was very important because it was the primary way to report on battlefield positions since there weren't satellites taking photos. The officer had to be able to sketch a situation quickly to send to his commander. Drawing, for Custer, was just as important as philosophy is now for someone interested in listening. Custer, however, never really recovered from his arrogance. I hope I can!

It's not too late. You don't have to be in a graduate program to read challenging material and really think about it.

You will begin to read philosophy when you really need to and not a minute before.

So the first step in the development of my philosophy of motivational listening was to be a reader of philosophy. I was always a reader, but this was taking the challenge to a new level. There's a certain sloppiness we're allowed when writing fiction, but not in expository writing. Still, fiction has a certain value I'll discuss later.

My journey begins with the examination of art. The nature of my work here is to examine the less scientific, more mystical nature of motivating others by listening to them, and I had a head start on thinking about art, because I was sculpting stone and making paintings long before I began to dig deep into coaching: listening as a conversational art form.

My basic conclusion after reading *Why Art Cannot Be Taught* was that Elkins was correct in saying that art cannot be taught because by definition, great artists make great art. *Great* means that something clicks in their heart, some sort of elusive X-Factor, and it usually includes leading new schools of thought which influence the world and also attaining a degree of fame or wealth. This has more to do with being at the right place at the right time than any sort of instruction one might follow or consume.

Elkins notes that any great artist learns to make art in almost any other way besides schooling. Since schooling couldn't claim to teach artists to be great, Elkins said that we might as well keep on teaching art at universities the way it had always been done. He identified a problem but had no proposed solution.

I decided that he was tragically incorrect in failing to offer a more excellent way to engage with art students. Coaching, I believed, and more generically any authentic community with leaders who motivate by listening, may not teach anyone to become a great artist as defined by fame or material wealth. But it could help artists to become well-adjusted people, less prone to isolation and even to suicide or self-medication—things which have been known to destroy artists in their prime. These things are avoidable, and so we may say that it's not guaranteed to make artists great, but it is designed to help them achieve their potential—which is all I've ever hoped to do for someone anyway!

What about the art of motivational listening: can it be taught? Since, philosophically, I am not sure if any art can be taught, the answer is no. However, I do believe it can be attained. There is a science of listening which can be studied like the science of mixing color. But just because you can mix red and yellow to get orange doesn't mean you can move people to action with your painting. Just because you can ask the standard questions, such as, "What do you hope to get out of this conversation?" doesn't mean you're going to become the greatest coach by standards of fame or wealth. Or, since the coach's career really isn't important, I should say, just because you know a few powerful questions doesn't mean your listening is going to be great and result in highly motivated people around you. Your own success or greatness isn't really even the goal when you're engaged in an art form like listening. That's the paradox. Greatness as a listener doesn't run on a scale the way great art does in Elkins' opinion. Greatness is attainable for everyone just as everyone can learn to pray or meditate. *You do not have to have natural talent to become a skilled listener!* Just as the instructors at West Point knew that anyone can learn to draw, so I believe that anyone can learn the basic skills to be a better listener.

The art, however, that is, the piece of listening that comes from the heart, cannot be taught. Perhaps it can be caught, like a ball or the common cold. It's infectious. The art is an art of getting out of the way. Getting out of the way of anything: an oncoming car, a baseball hurled at your head, the spotlight, all of these are reflexive. Learn the skills first, and your natural reflexes will turn listening into an art as you spend time thinking about it. I'm grateful to Mark Whitacre for pointing out in the foreword what I might not have even realized about myself: that I spend most of my waking moments thinking about how to help people become better at listening (myself included!). Because we are talking about unteachable reflexes as the highest form of artfulness, I work in a sideways manner, using metaphors to help you think about it, rather than an instructional tack. Tacking, for that matter, is a great way to think about it. A ship tacks on an angle in a zigzag pattern to make headway into a headwind. As we learn to motivate and listen, we too must tack. We must be willing to work sideways.

As Ronald Reagan said, "There's no limit to the amount of good you can do if you don't care who gets the credit." If you give up the credit, fade into the background, never get noticed for what you've done by anyone around you, well, that's the definition of a great listener. It's still an art that can't exactly be taught. But when you change the definition of "great" to include those who aren't rich or famous or breaking new ground by doing what they do, it opens the door to hope. You can become a great motivational listener. Something will have to click in your heart, which I can't teach but I can tack towards via metaphor. You'll also need a community to grow in which I can only model in the way I participate with several organizations (and offer by way of inviting you to comment on my blog).

The second question in my philosophy of listening is a much broader question in the world of philosophy. Are we listening for something specific? What will be helpful to listen for? If we want people to walk away from our conversation motivated, what will we have to hear? The word "motivation" is about being free to move based on their own motive. At best, we free people to move on their own—that's called "auto-motivation." Like an automobile, they're rolling down the street without a horse pulling it. We're not trying to push or pull anyone. We're just greasing the axles. If we want to motivate, we want to facilitate a well-oiled machine, free from rust, free from obstacle, free to grow and progress. How do we get this kind of freedom? "The truth will make you free."[2] So, first we look for something true, and after that, we trust the process.

But what is truth? Remember, this is a philosophy *of listening* so I'm not going to try to address the question in its entirety. I want to dig deep enough to think about truth in practical ways that improve my listening. I don't want to claim to be the sort of philosopher who spends a lifetime and writes a doctoral dissertation on truth. Still, I want to do a little better than some sort of fuzzy political truthiness. There's something to find here, and it is worth thinking about.

As a motivational listener, you'll be listening for truth too. But not so much in the way of a judge or lawyer in a courtroom. Instead, you're listening for the truth like a hunting guide looks for cougar spoor. Yep, the old biologist's joke is true: spoor happens. The real value of being a hunting guide is in recognizing the unexpected for what it is—that's a certain powerful sort of truth. If you were teaching people to hunt for deer here in northern Indiana, you'd think it's not so difficult to avoid the danger of you, the predator, becoming prey. Yet some years ago, perhaps around 2007, I was working in Ohio and picked up a newspaper which reported claims that several people spotted a cougar in their backyards or, as rural Ohioans call it, "the timber." Some of them saw paw prints, others heard cat yowls, and I can't remember for sure, but some may have even gotten a fuzzy photograph. Yet, in this article, a representative of the Ohio Department of Natural Resources was quoted as saying, "There are no cougars in Ohio."

Do not be alarmed, good people of Ohio, there are no cougars here.

Now, eight years later, there are many current articles about cougars in Ohio woodlands available on Google. As unusual and unexpected as they may have been in 2007, when they came back after a very long absence, even during those early days, you would do well to recognize the signs of this animal in your vicinity—and to be able to say to yourself the first time it happens, "I know there are no cougars, but here is evidence of a cougar, and there is the cougar" and to *take appropriate action.* Being able to recognize and take at face value something which is highly improbable is a key component to being a good hunting guide or listener. Recognizing the possibility of the improbable as a critical element of truth takes awareness and alertness. This is worth paying for if you're a hunter who employs a guide. You need a guide who doesn't say, "There are no cougars in Ohio" (or wherever you may be).

On the flipside of listening for the unexpected, there are things we may uncover as we listen like trackers looking for signs that could be helpful, things we hear as we listen to people's stories which could lead to discovery of something spectacular, perhaps even resulting in some sort of breakthrough, even, dare we say, greatness? To continue with the hunting guide analogy, this sort of attention to the unexpected could be the difference-maker and lead to knowing how to find not just any buck, but the 20-point buck; to not just locate the hole where any northern pike are hiding, but to catch a record fish. The signs are truths of what may be ahead. A major piece of the truths we look for are those things which have not yet happened but may have an extreme impact like freedom or greatness.

When looking for truth, you are looking for something you do not know. This is the core idea behind *Black Swan.* According to Taleb, the Black Swan event is "an *outlier,* as it lies outside the realm of regular expectations, because nothing in the past can convincingly point to its possibility. Secondly, it carries an extreme impact.... Third, in spite of its outlier status, human nature makes us concoct explanations for its occurrence *after* the fact, making it explainable and predictable.... It is easy to see that life is the cumulative effect of a handful of significant shocks.... Black Swan Logic makes *what you don't know* far more relevant than what you do know. Consider that many Black Swans can be caused and exacerbated *by their being unexpected*."[3]

This is what we're looking for when we listen. Where are the handful of shocks, positive or negative? To refer to an earlier essay where I discussed the nature of the knuckleball, say for example that you are the batter and the knuckleball pitcher makes a mistake. He throws a pitch that rotates, and the ball, rather than knuckling impossibly, suddenly becomes very hittable. The only problem is that you may be so surprised by the relative ease that you miss the pitch anyway.

Another pitch, even more rare than the poorly-thrown knuckleball, relies on the surprise. This pitch, called an Eephus pitch, is served up to the batter in such a way that it is intended to be so hittable that the batter misses.

"The delivery from the pitcher has very low velocity and usually catches the hitter off guard. Its invention is attributed to Rip Sewell of the Pittsburgh Pirates in the 1940s. According to manager Frankie Frisch, the pitch was named by outfielder Maurice Van Robays. When asked what it meant, Van Robays replied, 'Eephus ain't nothing, and that's a nothing pitch.'"[4] Although the origin is not known for certain, Eephus may come from the Hebrew word אפס (pronounced "EFF-ess") meaning "nothing."[5]

The Eephus pitch must be used with terrible infrequency— a complete outlier, a total Black Swan event. The minute it becomes expected, it becomes worthless. It's no longer a Black Swan event. Sometimes it's called a ball, sometimes a strike, usually makes the batter laugh, and fools even the umpire. Once, Ted Williams hit a home run in the All-Star Game on an Eephus pitch.

Ted Williams was the kind of batter who was always ready, because Ted was one of the greats. Ted Williams was ready for everything, even the highly improbable. And so his probability of hitting was high. I do not think Ted Williams would have said, "There are no cougars in Ohio."

Figure 3. "Buddy" Balogh of the Elkhart County Railroaders Vintage Base Ball Club hurls an "Eephus" pitch. Photo courtesy of Norma "Mother Hen" Barrera-Miles.

Human greatness in terms of "no limits to what may be accomplished," is often the result of flexibly and appropriately responding to a Black Swan event when it happens, as it happens. It means the ability to recognize cougar spoor and get out of the woods, or being ready for the Eephus pitch, that moment in which things become so surprisingly easy for you to knock it out of the park that you're likely to completely miss your chance. I think the worst thing we could do when we see the Eephus pitch coming is to freeze. Better to swing away and miss than not to try at all; or as Alfred, Lord Tennyson famously penned, "Better to have loved and lost than never to have loved at all."

The issue becomes one of preparation. How do you seize the day, pick up the book or ask for that date if you aren't awake? Again, the quest is not only for the truth of what is now. It's also for the truth of what might be possible even if it has never been done, seen or thought of. This is where freedom and greatness exists, and yes, it's improbable, but partly because you aren't looking for it.

I can teach the science of listening, but not the art, simply because it is an art, and must become reflexive. I don't know what surprises *you* will be listening for, but you have to use your heart and stay alert!

❖ When was the last time you had an unanticipated event, how did you react?

❖ How can you prepare yourself to react to an unanticipated event, whether positive or negative: in your career, in your family, in your charitable work?

Facts vs. fiction

So far, we've established that some of the truths we are looking for include those things which may be highly improbable but also very impacting. They are things we don't yet know, but they are true. Tomorrow is full of things that are true which we don't yet know. Like a guide looking for unexpected signs, there are pieces of truth which can help if we pick up on them quickly.

The second thing a motivational listener is tuned in for is a principle. Principles are important because they are "a fundamental truth, law, doctrine or *motivating force.*"[6]

A principle of motivational listening is this: A principle functioning as a motivating force for someone is all you have to find and highlight if you want to drive the unstoppable armored car of motivation to the bank and make a deposit which will come back with interest.

So how do you arrive at principles? By pointing out the facts? Usually not. Facts are often misleading or distracting. Even if facts prove something, they don't motivate nearly as well as a good story because facts never illuminate a principle as well as a story can. You need that principle lit up like the Statue of Liberty on the Fourth of July.

When my son Benjamin was only six years old, I took him to Dairy Queen. He's my third son, the one I call my ninja-philosopher. At the time, he was on a jag where he wore a ninja sweatshirt nonstop. Also, he's always ambushing me with little philosophical moments, and this one came out of the blue as usual:

"You know, Dad," he said, chowing on a sundae with the most matter-of-fact attitude, "there's no such thing as fiction, because whenever you write a story, it creates a new galaxy somewhere in the universe and that galaxy is now real: like *Star Wars*."

Wait a second. Is *Star Wars* real?

Yes, it is.

> *Questions of the authenticity of imaginings invite answers, and yet may remain unanswered. For the imagination is not always subject to immediate proof or demonstration. It is often subject only to the slow and partial authentication of experience. It is subject, that is, to a practical, though not an exact, validation, and it is subject to correction. For a work of imagination to endure through time, it must prove valid, and it must survive correction. It is correctable by experience, by critical judgment, and by further works of imagination.*
>
> *To say that a work of imagination is subject to correction is, of course, to imply that there is no "world of imagination" as distinct from or opposed to the "real world." ... one of the most profound of human needs is for the truth of imagination to prove itself in every life and place in the world, and*

for the truth of the world's lives and places to be proved in imagination.[7]
—Wendell Berry

I conceded that Benjamin was on to something. Just because something isn't factual doesn't mean it doesn't bear witness to something authentic, real: the seed of truth, a principle.

Israel's King David was a "candidate for a wax job" in 2 Samuel 12, so, rather than point out the facts for him, his old friend, Nathan, came to tell him a story instead:

> *There were two men in a certain city, the one rich and the other poor. The rich man had very many flocks and herds; but the poor man had nothing but one little ewe lamb, which he had bought. And he brought it up, and it grew up with him and with his children; it used to eat of his morsel, and drink from his cup, and lie in his bosom, and it was like a daughter to him. Now there came a traveler to the rich man, and he was unwilling to take one of his own flock or herd to prepare for the wayfarer who had come to him, but he took the poor man's lamb, and prepared it for the man who had come to him.*
> —2 Samuel 12:1b–4a

Once David condemned the man in the story on principle, Nathan pointed out that David was the rich man. At this point, David, who liked the facts and only the facts, said, "Hey, man, you tricked me with a fake story. It was all lies! I thought this was a REAL case you asked me to try." No, no he didn't. "David said to Nathan, 'I have sinned against the Lord.'"[8]

David understood that even if Nathan's story was a "work of imagination," it's not distinct from or opposed to the "real world."

Almost all Jesus' discourse in small groups came in the form of narrative. He made up stories. Is The Prodigal Son[9] real? As far as we know, it doesn't contain a single fact.

It is important for a motivational listener to learn to appreciate narrative, to read fiction, because the element of truth found within fiction is primarily based on true principles as opposed to the focus of non-fiction which bases its quest for truth on the accuracy of facts (oh, what a tedious effort that makes a book like this one for a big fat liar like me). When we are listening, our job is to be on the lookout for principles and allow the speaker to discern which principles they will apply. *Just the facts, ma'am* won't get you very far. Facts are OK. I don't stop people while they tell me the facts. But I'm not in a courtroom to judge a case. Usually, as listeners we are in a movie theater looking for a bit of heroism to cheer or a villain to condemn, just the way David did.

Fiction may contain much truth even as it lies. In getting at the principle, in lighting up the truth, fiction is a more powerful tool than fact.

Conversely, facts (statistics) are often used to obfuscate truth and can just as easily cause the fruit they might have borne to rot. We see this all the time in our political journalism. Every statistic can be useful to prove someone's agenda, and probably will be. Empirical evidence is dying to be interpreted.

So, the second piece of my philosophy of listening is this: if you want to be a great listener, read a novel. Find books that make you laugh and cry and think about human nature, work at identifying principles. I consider it cross-training.

❖ List at least four fiction books you will read in the next 12 months. Do not include business parables. We are looking for books that aren't driving toward a specific point or agenda for the reader to learn.

Article 8

Facts vs. fiction episode II: Return of the Jedi listener

Truly wonderful, the mind of a child is.
—Yoda

If truth is broader than the facts of the matter, is there danger that we might be led astray by a story? What, are we gods now that we have begun to make up fictitious stories and add, like pantheists, to the dimensions of truth? I had wondered with at least some worry and concern that if we are created in God's image, then when we writers create a new "galaxy," as Benjamin put it, are we then taking the role of a god in that galaxy? When we create, one might say we're playing god, and that seems dangerous at first glance. I don't want to be responsible for creating my own truth out of nothing. So the next thing I asked my son Benjamin at Dairy Queen that day was:

"Benji, when we create a new story, who is the god in that new galaxy?"

Without a moment's hesitation, he replied, "The God we pray to." (His tone said, "Duh, dad, who else would be god but God?")

Let's "turn and become like children" by taking Benjamin's perception at face value because the kingdom of heaven belongs to people who perceive the world like this.[10]

But where is God in *Star Wars?* In Lucas' yin-yang-ish fantasy world, the "Force", the protagonist, and the antagonist are all needed for the universe to have balance, but Darth Vader is still bad and Luke Skywalker is still a good guy (we'll get to good guys later). And yet, according to Benjamin, in the *Star Wars* Galaxy, the Force is not god, nor is George Lucas. Only God is God. Truth in the "real world" is truth in imagination, and that's how we *know* Darth Vader is bad. We can understand this (perhaps we understand it better than we ever will later) when we are six years old. So when I talk about stories in which truth is displayed, I'm talking about what Wendell Berry says "is correctable by experience, by critical judgment, and by further works of imagination."[11]

In other words, there is that within us which can either find something resonant or discordant within a story by which we can judge that story, as King David did[12], and as do all children the moment they begin to watch *Star Wars.* Our ability to recognize truth, collectively over time, is a reflection of God in the entire known and imagined universe.

The ability to find truth in stories that haven't yet been written is evidence of expanding truth. This is the truth that anything could happen in the future, and, though it's a little more complicated, anything could have happened in the past. This expanding truth is the truth of potential. It's a critical thing for the motivational listener to recognize.

The universe itself is said to be expanding. More people live on this world today than yesterday, and more will be here tomorrow, each living a reality which grows bigger each day as more and more people experience it. Think of it like water. As each day solidifies into reality, truth expands like water freezing. The potential truth expands to cover what is happening as it locks into something as concrete as yesterday.

A lot of people have trouble with Jesus' statement, "I am the way, and the truth, and the life"[13] because it sounds so finite, so ... narrow. And it is narrow; he said, "For the gate is narrow and the way is hard, that leads to life, and those who find it are few."[14] It is a contractive truth, like a muscle flexing its power, like ice melting in a river which explodes and pushes everything before it; and it is contractual, so that those of us who recognize it find we are happiest when we abide by the limitations of its statutes. But this narrowness is not so limiting as it first appears. The muscle has no power without an ability to relax. People who take *I am the Truth* as evidence of a tight permanent contraction will find that their spiritual muscles cramp up, they're asking for spasms.

Just because I say that truth is expanding does not mean it is not also contracting. I simply think that we spend far too much energy trying to make it contractual and contractive for those around us and never enough time helping people find the ways in which it is expansive. A strong muscle is a flexible muscle. Usually we look like a guy who does bodybuilding for competition: he's over-flexed but under-flexible, and strong as he may seem, he's unable really to compete in any sort of athletic endeavors other than the bodybuilding competition itself. Following the regimen of becoming a bodybuilder has prepared him for nothing but further following of that regimen. We are listening as truth expands for opportunities to make a decathlete of those we motivate and listen to. (I don't mean offense by this to bodybuilders; I assume they are aware of what their bodies are honed to do and what they aren't able to do as well.)

I think that if the universe is expanding in possibilities, then all the possibilities that truth encompasses is expanding too. Possibilities of what might be true, improbable as they seem beforehand, later become part of reality: Columbus was so locked into finding the Indies, it took a while for people to recognize that he'd found something else, something, we might say, even less probable than a round-earth shortcut to India. European culture at the time was also so deeply focused on his identity as an explorer that somehow they missed the idea that Columbus didn't really discover anything that wasn't already known by someone. But one principle of exploration is that once we begin to explore, looking for something improbable, there are plenty of opportunities to find other things that weren't probable as well. We have to explore! We have to believe there is more to truth, not less! We have to find a way to walk on a narrow path and see it for the route of immense potential that it is.

I had a conversation with a family friend this summer. Joe (not his real name) is a successful attorney. If I listed some of the clients he has, you'd recognize them from incidents in the national news over the past three years. Joe was willing to chat about anything; I wish we'd had all day.

We're just chatting about literature or whatever strikes our fancy and then I dropped the words "absolute truth" in the conversation and Joe stopped me cold.

"Hold it. What do you mean when you say *absolute truth*?" Joe went on to explain that his definition of "truth" is "the most accurate possible picture of reality." *Reality* is the age old picture of the blind men trying to describe the elephant by touching its ear, tail or leg. None of us has a full picture, but there is something concrete we're getting at upon which we can all agree.

That's what you want in court, Joe; it's what you want when determining who broke the window, or whether or not your spouse is cheating, or whether or not a goal is attainable by a certain date, or what you want when exploring *REALITY* in the GROW model, yes, most of the time, it's what you want. That thing upon which we can all agree, that informs decisions in a quite sane way.

Thanks to Joe's challenge, I've had to think long and hard about using the word "absolute" in this context. I was considering using the term "absolute" for that infinitely expanding possibility aspect of truth. But upon reflection, a better word for what I'm getting at is really just "expanding." So let's use "absolute" in this discussion in the way you're familiar with: that ever-narrower version of events which blocks us into a corner. *I shot the sheriff, but I did not shoot the deputy.* Even that absolute depiction of events still requires some sort of explanation.

The quest for recognizing and reacting to Black Swan events has to do with expanding truth, not narrowing it down to an absolute. Remember that what we know is never as important as what we don't know. We know that "Jesus is the truth" but we also have to recognize that this isn't a limiting factor—not an absolute in that way. Instead, to see it as an ever-expanding version of reality keeps us from putting God or the Scriptures in a box and taping the lid shut so we can take it along with us like a teddy bear. Experiencing Jesus as absolute truth is a teddy bear; it has few implications and mostly gives us comfort in knowing (or thinking we know) all that needs to be known. Hey. Knowing everything is a pretty big turnoff, especially to Jesus. Experiencing Jesus as expanding truth is a real cougar in Ohio. This sort of truth keeps coming back to places where it has been exterminated, but it has range, it also reaches farther into the unknown. It has implications and is worth watching for. And it's exciting.

Absolute truth, then, would be an ever-narrowing definition of reality, more and more focused on those things we can

KNOW as REALITY. But as my attorney friend pointed out, whatever you think can actually be known with a certainty, any lawyer worth their salt can cast doubt upon in a jiffy. But expanding truth is the opposite, and a far more exciting quest. It's motivating, and it's pretty hard to cast doubt upon the aspect of truth that lives in our imaginations. Oh, someone may tell you it can't be done, but your imagination says you can build an MLM (multi-level marketing) empire. The fun thing about expanding truth is that it will only narrow in the future.

Then what happens to the idea of truth when we include the realm of imagination in our picture of reality? Is this the makings of insanity? Or, do we actually come closer to defining truth when we work at it in the other direction—not by narrowing our definition of truth but by broadening it to include all possible realities? And what benefit does that have for those who we hope to motivate as we listen to the quest for expanding truth in their lives?

We usually stumble over absolute truth because it has normally meant that we narrowly define reality as one sequence of events to the exclusion of all others, rather than thinking of it as an expanding of the possibilities of reality. In the realm of expanding truth, there are more dimensions than what we see, there are stories we've yet to uncover, there are heavens where our deepest desires are fulfilled (if playing harps and wearing haloes doesn't suit your fancy of the afterlife, then what does? Imagine it!), and hells which terrify us worse than any writer before Dante and Edgar Allan Poe and even after Steven King could ever dream up for us. There are, perhaps, extra-terrestrial beings, spirits evil, good and benign, and alternative histories and futures: What if Hitler had won and 70 years later the Nazis still ruled Europe, or more? What if Abram hadn't bedded Hagar? What if Jesus had explained truth to Pilate? What if Judas hadn't betrayed Jesus? What if the United States hadn't revolted from the British Crown? What if Lumumba hadn't been assassinated? What if Hiroshima hadn't happened—what if the Southern states had seceded?

How are the many possible answers to all these questions not part of truth? Can the idea of expanding truth include all the possibilities of what could be, or could have been, as well as what is?

It is in the possibilities of alternative futures that we find our path to greatness as motivational listeners.

Each of these possibilities of what might have been can speak to (but are not) the reality our courts seek, but they also speak to the reality our hearts hope to one day see. Like absolute power which (expands continually and) corrupts absolutely, expanding truth expands possibilities absolutely, which is why I was initially inclined to simply redefine "absolute truth." Semantically, however, it became a stumbling block.

Some coaches utilize visualization: Imagine yourself with a million dollars. What do you do with it? Cut out pictures from a magazine of how your life will look. Where will you go? Who will you help?

Can your imagination really predict and create your reality in the future—create an alternative and positive future? Can you literally carve a new reality out of this version of truth?

We've seen it work. But not always. We pray for healing and someone dies. We visualize millions, and remain locked in poverty. That is truth too, because it's reality too, to recognize that what we create in our imagination doesn't always materialize.

Yes, we've seen that happen, and on the other hand, God is still the God of the imagination, and of the future reality. So, what we imagine, or pray for, may be allowed to come to fruition, and it may not, and we may never get an explanation. As Peter said, "God is no respecter of persons"[15] when Peter's own possibilities expanded exponentially after a vision (he was shown that he was allowed to eat much more than what he previously thought, a metaphor for God's grace expanded to far more people than Peter previously presumed "chosen"). He would have preferred (until that day) that God would respect his reality, which was, after all, founded upon what humans thought God wanted, even commanded. Instead, he found that anything could be, even though not everything will be. Visualize as you may, sometimes your dreamed-for possibilities will enter the world we know as reality, and sometimes they won't. Sometimes your limitations get blown up. This is critical to encouragement: invite people to seek expanding possibilities, to imagine, but don't forget that not all those things we encounter in the realm of expanding truth will come down the funnel into the simpler, objective truth of the present reality. The absolute truth is that you, dear reader, could become rich and famous tomorrow, amen, let it be. The plain ol' truth is that you probably won't, and amen, let it be.

At six years old, Benjamin saw that fiction contains elements and principles of truth, and that absolute universal truth extends into every fictional world we could possibly create. If I create a fantasy world with a hateful god, I have written a tragedy, and our hearts recognize it as such because it defies a larger truth (as Wendell Berry would put it, we "correct" it). If I write of a dystopia like *The Matrix* where people have forgotten what love is in favor of social order and numbness, again: a tragedy. If I write of a world where things are not as they appear, where everything is a veneer, it's cause for revolt in our gut. If our hero is victorious, we rejoice. "That was a *good* movie," we say. *Anna Karenina* was depressing. "I think I'll take a break from Russian writers again," I said. Our desire for story comes from a hunger for the redemption we experience when our characters find truth or love, because "the God we pray to" as Benjamin said, has baked these expanding truths not only into our factual world, but by extension into our fictional ones. Truth is what we see in reality, but expanding truth we can only intuit.

We don't need to fear that a story will lead us astray. When writing fiction, I try very hard not to say what I think *should be said.* That would be a religious capitulation, propaganda, or worse. It falls short of the possibilities I could reach if I went after expanding truth. Instead, I trust my gut. When inviting people to expound, to expand upon what truth might be, we also need to invite them to push beyond what they think they *should say.*

A creative approach to motivation demands that we invite the creation of a story that builds a new reality, a galaxy wherein our speaker can find a principle that contains the seeds of truth, emotional seeds which can be planted upon their new planet to bear the fruit which will become a new fact—but not so that they become a statistic. Precisely because the new facts about them will make them legendary, mythical, epic in proportion to the sum of their own deeds and events. Or, in the event that their visualization does not create the new reality they hope for, we are a spotter, we are the net. Get back on the trapeze, up on the high wire, push for the new personal best again.

In our imaginations, we don't play God, we mirror God. In mirroring God, we touch the corner of the garments of expanding truth. I write a chapter in a novel and a voice says, "Who touched me?"

Is it possible that within the many faceted diamond of possibilities of expanding truth I could even find healing?

❖ What have you learned in the last 12 months that added to your expanding understanding of truth?

❖ Where are you exploring the edges of truth now, pushing the limits of your comfort zone?

Article 9

A garden gnome

O nce upon a time, there was a simple garden gnome named Bill (not his real name). Bill was a kindly looking type of gnome with a pipe and half-glasses he used for reading. It wasn't so much that he was looking down his nose at you, as he was looking over his cheeks. Of course, he wore a red cap and a green vest except on Tuesdays when he wore his plaid one. Bill the Gnome knew all the woodland creatures by name.

Figure 4. Bill the Gnome relaxing in his garden on a non-Tuesday.

Hubert the Turtle, Wally the Rabbit... Bill even had tea with Guinevere the Red Fox on occasion. His best friends lived underground. Andre the Mole would sit with Bill and play Scrabble until the sun came up. One sunny morning as he strolled along the hedgerow, he came across an old copy of "The Wind in the Willows" upside down in a patch of ferns. "I know," said Bill, "I'll take this over to Nancy the Field-mouse. She'll love this story." So off

he waddled, to find Mrs. Nancy, without even stop-
ping to wonder who might have lost this beautiful
book. And so his adventure began.

≈∘∾

I have for some time now had a theory that reading fiction would make one a better listener. But here's some exciting research that maybe doesn't prove it, but certainly shows a correlation, so don't take it from me. When it comes to social sciences, I'm no academic. I'm just a simple practitioner of empathy and fiction. But some folks discovered that fiction does indeed increase empathy—and even more importantly, reading nonfiction may even be a negative indicator!

≈∘∾

Those of us who are called upon to narrate
such stories have an omniscient view of the forest
where Bill lives, so that I, and now, by extension,
you, can quickly realize that the volume Bill found
was something Old Gravel-Pit the Snow Owl had
dropped one night. He'd been reading by the light
of the moon when he saw something far below his
treetop perch that caught his attention. It glistened
as though it were a very large rodent with one eye
open and the other eye closed. Was some cheeky
woodchuck winking at him? How dare he? And so,
forgetting his book, Old Gravel-Pit (we have long
forgotten how he came by this name. I suppose
that somewhere along the line they added the
"Old" part, though perhaps he was born with it, be-

ing an owl and all) and ... Where was I? Oh—and forgetting and dropping!—his book he swooped down to take what was rightfully his; that is, anything he sees, as far as he is concerned, be it a woodchuck or a pocket watch.

ॐ∙ॐ

Here is part of the abstract from a paper by Raymond A. Mar, et al, in the *Journal of Research in Personality*:

"While frequent readers are often stereotyped as socially awkward, this may only be true of non-fiction readers and not readers of fiction. Comprehending characters in a narrative fiction appears to parallel the comprehension of peers in the actual world, while the comprehension of expository non-fiction shares no such parallels. Frequent fiction readers may thus bolster or maintain their social abilities unlike frequent readers of non-fiction. . . . In general, fiction print-exposure positively predicted measures of social ability, while non-fiction print-exposure was a negative predictor. The tendency to become absorbed in a story also predicted empathy scores."[16]

ॐ∙ॐ

Of course it turned out to be a pocket watch some careless gnome had dropped; it would go nicely with a plaid vest for special times like Tues-

days. Old Gravel-Pit the Snow Owl was disgusted to find that it was both inedible and also useless at telling any sort of story. He went in search of his book again the next evening as the sun went down, and it was just at that same moment when Bill the Gnome turned out of the woods and into the field, so that aloft, Old Gravel-Pit finally saw his book waddling along. Without thinking how the book might be moving along the ground on its own, he snagged it in one talon. Poor surprised Bill forgot to let go of "The Wind in the Willows" as it lifted off, and soon he realized that he didn't want to let go of it anymore, now, being so high off the ground, and up he went, higher and higher, sailing towards the Great Wheat Field where one could get lost, and beyond! "What dangers we face when we hang on to something too tightly without thinking!" so thought Bill. "But if it's a book like 'The Wind in the Willows,' it may just be worth it! Why, there may be IDEAS in here I haven't thought of for some time." The breeze tickled his toes, and so even as his stubby fingers grew sore, he determined that he would follow the flight of this book no matter where it might lead him.

Do you feel for Bill? What would you rather do, read more about Bill, or go find this study online and read that? Did you really read the abstract, or just skim it? Did you just jump ahead absorbed in the story to read more about the silly gnome? (If so, it's a good sign for you as an empathetic person and for me as a writer!) Now, I'm not saying that this little story I slapped out in a few minutes about a gnome and an owl contains any sort of literary brilliance, but the truth is, we hunger for story (which gives us something to think about) more than we do for non-fiction (which is where we get told what to think). Chances are you aren't reading this essay while on a date. No, of course, you go to a movie!

At the bottom of the study, the researchers concluded that while there is a direct correlation between empathy and reading of fiction (but a negative correlation between empathy and those more familiar with non-fiction), they weren't yet able to determine cause. In other words, did reading fiction make people more empathetic, or are more empathetic people naturally attracted to reading fiction? It's unclear. One thing we do know is that fewer people (and gnomes) are reading fiction all the time.

❖ Go find a children's book and a child and read to them. Think of your own questions to ask the child afterward.

Article 10

Listeners and all facts

The listener understands that truth may contain facts, but no true story contains all facts, and therefore a motivational listener is unconcerned with knowing all facts. Long before Christ walked the earth, Lao Tzu spoke of the "myriad things" or "ten-thousand things" while Solomon ridiculed the quest for all facts by saying "And there is nothing new under the sun.... For all is vanity and a striving after wind."[17] The aim of their poetic philosophy is to uncover principle, not to catalog fact. They realized long before computers existed that nobody would ever be able to collect all facts in one place and that facts were, in fact, relatively superfluous to the discovery and illumination of truth.

❖ What do you not need to know in order to move forward? What will it take to forge ahead and leave the gap in your knowledge behind?

Article 11

On story and memory

M otivational listeners leverage the power of emotions tied to memory.

In courtroom psychology where facts are king, memory has been shown to be one of the most unreliable tools for discovery.[18] Each time we recall an event, our brains add to or subtract from the experience, creating a patina, adding layers of varnish or grime so that while the antique table of our memories looks less and less like it did the day that memory was made, we only recognize it years later as the shiny antique we now see.

Let's play a little more with that idea. If an ancient memory in our head is like an antique table, what is the value of stripping it back to its bare facts? For those who love the PBS[19] show *Antiques Roadshow,* you know that stripping the patina and refinishing a piece of old furniture actually lessens the value of it, but in some cases, a painting or piece of furniture can also be restored by an expert giving it even greater value. In the same way, your memory coated over with layers, may become less valuable as a tool to illuminate beauty and principle if stripped by confrontation with the basic facts; as if it were a pearl stripped back to the initial grain which irritated the oyster. On the other hand, the idea of "clean-

Figure 5. Antique table, as seen on the Internet.

ing or restoring" corresponds to the idea that we might take that memory and distill from it the underlying principle, making it elegant again.

We do not want to strip the memory to bare facts, but we do want to highlight the beauty of what we learned from it, what stays with us as evidence of the refining of time which makes it more valuable. It isn't the wood of the table (though it may be from an extinct tree such as the American chestnut— that is the like the last remaining person whose personal memory includes World War I). The beauty is the wood *plus* the patina itself, something no human could create, it's only made by time.

Memories attached to emotions are one of the most relia-ble tools for getting at the principles of what impact events have had on the speaker's life. My memories of Congo are not perhaps factual, but the principles I've drawn highlight what was valuable in the experience and display the burls, knots, and grain of how those memories formed me.

We might even say that the writers of the four gospels who waited some 30 years, may not have given us the same facts, in the strictest sense, that they might have if they were involved in some sort of daily journalism during the days of Christ. On the other hand, their somewhat delayed picture may be even more valuable for the patina the time lapse added; the things Matthew and John remembered because of how the principles continued to ring true over time come closer to an illumination of reality (or, the truth of what had happened) than what a newspaper man might have given us had he written about Christ's doings on October 2, and then again on the fourth and ninth.

Humanity has been intrigued by the rapid consumption of facts on a daily basis for some time. But to what end? Where is the value in newly minted fact? After the school shooting in Ore-gon, a friend of mine noted that often people spit out emotional blogs without even having the facts. "At first," he said, "the news came that 12 were dead, 20 injured. It wasn't even close. It was only 9 dead." I told him I did think that it was relatively close. I reminded him that we all blog as soon as possible to drive traffic to our blogs with links, for example, to the president's speech. (That's how we're told to market our blogs.) I realized it was a pretty lousy reason to jump on the mass-shooting online feeding frenzy, to be sure. I felt ashamed because while in my own state of emotional distress, sick at heart at what our culture continues to accept, yet I had done this. We know there is no news. We can talk about this sickness in our culture any day.

> *For my part, I could easily do without the post-office... I never received more than one or two letters in my life ... that were worth the postage... To a philosopher, all news, as it is called, is gossip, and they who edit and read it are old women over their tea... As for Spain, for instance, if you know how to throw in Don Carlos and the Infanta, and Don Pedro, and Seville and Granada, from time to time in the right proportions—they may have changed the names a little since I saw the papers—and serve up a bull-fight when other entertainments fail, it will be true to the letter, and give us as good an idea of the exact state or ruin of things in Spain as the most succinct and lucid reports ... in the newspaper: and as for England, almost the last significant scrap of news from that quarter was the revolution of 1649; and if you have learned the history of her crops for an average year, you never need attend to that thing again.[20]*
>
> —Henry David Thoreau

What is "true to the letter" and the fascination and thirst for it is the exact problem Thoreau identified. We "live this mean life," he said, "because our vision does not penetrate the surface of things."[21] The facts themselves are the surface of things—it's that bare, clean, new surface which as yet bears no patina of memory over time. I think most of what we look at is impenetrable precisely because it's new enough and it hasn't developed depth.

The listener hears stories constructed from memory knowing that such stories are, as time goes on, scientifically unreliable in terms of factual reconstruction of events, but that the same memory is remarkably reliable in its ability to recall emotions experienced or established during an event and illustrate the principle the speaker is able to take away. For example, in my recollections of Zaire 27 years ago, my memory has such a patina that you should not trust my memory to give you a perfect rendering of the facts. I have to look things up if I want the facts. What year was Burleigh A. Law killed by the rebels? 1969, I think. (It was 1964. Why was I thinking 1969? My father was there in '69 and it wasn't even a dangerous place to be any more, the rebellion was over.) You should be able to trust that the patina on my memory will give you a very accurate rendition of how the events *felt and shaped my life.* This allows a listener to penetrate the surface of things.

Perhaps I remembered the facts incorrectly because I felt that my Dad *was* in danger years earlier, in the 60s! I can tell you for sure that there were times in 1987–88 that I thought *I was, possibly, in danger in Zaire! That if things somehow went wrong, I, too, could be shot in Wembo Nyama.* That is how I felt. In fact, on my third draft of this essay, I began to wonder, *do I have some lingering PTSD?* I grabbed my copy of *Debriefing Aid Workers and*

Missionaries: A Comprehensive Manual and skimmed through it again. But I'm not sure anyone has ever debriefed someone 27 years after their cross-cultural experience. There is a seven-step process for Critical Incident Debriefing which begins with introductions and "The Facts about the Experience" and moves on to thoughts, sensory impressions and emotions, and so on. Twenty-seven years after the fact, I'm not sure any of the so-called facts will be remotely accurate, but the values I picked up are engrained in my life for good.

Learning from life means drawing principles we can connect deeply with because of the beauty of our emotional patina. Emotions are the patina on memory that makes it a valuable antique. And they're more valuable than the facts because you can draw on their wisdom for future action, for purpose in life. So listen carefully and see the emotions and memories together as something more valuable than the facts.

❖ What memories do you have that have created a motivational factor in your life regardless of whether or not you even remember the details factually?

❖ How do the emotions of these memories drive you?

❖ When was the last time someone shared a story with you in which you thought that they probably had the facts wrong but you saw that it was moving them to some sort of action (positive or negative)?

❖

❖ What happens when you really listen to the feelings behind the memory?

Article 12

How listeners read the Bible

T he listener reads fiction with abandon, uncovering truth wherever it may be found, and reads non-fiction with caution recognizing that each fact stacked upon another fact could be building a tower of Babel; that a large collection of facts twisted for someone's profit are like polling results used in a political campaign. This is less valuable to you than a single principle uncovering some broad truth. You can figure out an agenda for yourself so that you can apply the principle.

And so it is for people concerned about reading the books of the Bible. If you take them to be fiction (or less-than-factual), you should be able to read them with abandon and just enjoy applying the principles you find. To me this is a non-threatening invitation to people who don't believe it.

On the other hand, if you think of these disparate books collectively known as the Bible as a non-fiction anthology full of facts, read them with caution knowing that the conclusion you reach has deep implications for everything you do because facts must be interpreted correctly or you'll be worse off than you were before you found those facts. You're under the gun to find the *correct* interpretation. As the Ethiopian eunuch said in Acts 8:31, "How can I [understand the prophets] unless someone guides me?"

You can find principles in any novel on your own but in a book with claims on the truth, you need a guide or you are bound to mess up.

Similarly, when you listen to a companion telling a story, encourage their wildest fantasies and take their statements of fact with a grain of salt.

Canonized books of story or poetry, when they are used as factual sledgehammers, cause trauma, but their original impact in society was due to their usefulness in the way their story elucidated truth regardless of any concern for factuality. "Factuality" is a modern western construct. The first question to ask when studying canonic texts is not, "Is this or that a fact?" but rather, "How does this story impact me emotionally? What true principles are here?"

Forensics came to the United States in 1904. Seven years later, the first conviction was handed out because of a fingerprint match. In a Radley Balko story, I found that crime lab analysts are *"paid per conviction."* Their incentive to misguide a jury as expert testifiers was ethically out of line. He quotes Michael Saks, a law professor at Arizona State University: "Judges have no scientific training. They're trained in legal analysis, not scientific analysis. The fundamental problem with forensics and the criminal justice system is that legal thinking and scientific thinking just aren't compatible."[22]

To a similar degree, thinking and applying principles and judging a story based on whether it contains facts is the same sort of problem.

❖ What story from the Bible (if you don't believe in the factuality of the Bible) or from another ancient myth or text (if you do believe in the factuality of the Bible) impacts you emotionally?

Article 13

Why leaders read fiction

Self-reflection: Because literary fiction uses techniques that dislocate our minds and call our attention to strangeness in the world (called *foregrounding*) that may lead us to be unsettled and look at things differently (*de-familiarization*) which interacts with *stillness*. This includes self-contemplation and appreciation of art (which I believe is a component of what I've called *hedgerows*, discussed later on) and causes self-reflection.

Empathy: Kidd and Castano propose that by prompting readers to take an active writerly role to form representations of characters' subjective states, literary fiction recruits Theory of Mind. "More broadly, [our experiments] suggest that Theory of Mind may be influenced by engagement with works of art."[23] In other words, fiction may increase empathy—both accurately identifying peoples' emotions cognitively, but also giving us the flexibility to place ourselves in their shoes (affective empathy). There is some indication that reading fiction helps us suspend judgment of others.

Goal Setting: This one surprised me. "According to Oatley ...narrative fiction constitutes simulation that runs our 'planning-processor,' that is, the part of our minds we use in daily life to plan actions in order to attain goals."[24]

The academics have much more work to do, but the more studies they do, the more links they find between reading literary fiction and several of the major pieces we need to become really good motivational listeners.

Keith Oatley famously said that "fiction is twice as true as fact."[25] I believe that this idea is related to my concept of "expanded truth" in that by extending our possible world views, we broaden truth's possibilities, rather than narrowing it.

All these papers have one major commonality: they all acknowledge that there isn't definitive proof of cause. When it comes to encouraging the reading of literature for the sake of improving empathy, some major issues come up. What's your personality type? How do you define "literature?" Does your empathic personality predispose you to reading, or does reading really cause empathy? There are a lot of outstanding questions.

Here's one more statement I found interesting:

> *Because fiction gives us a low-threat context, it gives us an optimal aesthetic distance for constructive content simulation.*[26]

In 2011 and 2012 as I finished my first novel, our financial situation was treacherous. (What, you've never heard of a first-time novelist who's broke?) There were days it seemed it would be easier to just ditch everything, get in my car and leave my family behind. It wasn't that my wife and I were having problems, certainly not that we had fights or marital issues, in general, but perhaps the best way to put it was that I felt pretty strongly that I wasn't helping our situation, and no matter what I tried, I couldn't seem to shake that for a long time. The character in that novel named Arnold, who leaves his wife and young children and goes to Alaska, was for me as a writer, *constructive content simulation.* I was able to enter the world of a man who leaves his wife from a safe *aesthetic distance* which allowed me to engage my "planning processor" and think through the ramifications of such activity experiencing it virtually without doing something destructive. None of the research I've read says anything about *writing* fiction. But it seems to have done the same thing for me. The immersion for the writer is, in many ways, far deeper than it is for the reader. The writer has to read the work dozens of times over, correcting it for authenticity as much as possible (because works of imagination are correctible and the last thing the novelist wants to happen is to be corrected immediately and often on something trivial. We're much more interested in being told "your dialog was real"). This means the "planning processor" mode works overtime.

Sometimes it feels as though that planning processor, like a microchip, is at risk of overheating. It occurs to me now that this sort of overheating may be one cause of writer's block: the point of saturation. So, be aware of saturation as well. Sometimes the listener is working too hard, reading too much, over-thinking their world. And sometimes, the person we're listening to may be doing it, too.

Read. But don't over-saturate yourself.

❖ Who do you admire as a person of self-reflection, empathy, or goal setting? What could you learn from them?

Article 14

Going to the edge of the world from the middle of nowhere

The calamity of the information age is that the toxicity of data increases much faster than its benefits.[27]
—Nassim Nicholas Taleb

A t the edge of the world, we are known. In the middle of nowhere, we are lost.

In 2005 I visited friends in Senegal: we'll call them Phil, Laurie, their three kids and Grandma Betty. Phil had spent several years of free time building a 12' sailboat with hand tools. Betty sewed the sail by hand. Phil stored his boat at a rustic resort run by an old Frenchman. The campground was built on a sandbar on the Atlantic Ocean south of St. Louis, Senegal. Between the sandbar and the mainland was an estuary lagoon about three-quarters mile wide, and this was where we sailed Phil's boat. It was too small for the Atlantic, but the waves in the lagoon on a nice day were like sailing on a lake.

Figure 6. The sailboat.

Figure 7. Author detailing a picture of a dolphin on the bow.

The sandbar resort had Mauritanian tents for cabins—cement block walls about four feet high with a broad canvas stretched over top so that the ocean breeze could slip in and keep you cool. It was windy enough that bugs were not a problem; hot during the day of course, but at night, cool, around 70 degrees. The bathhouses were like what you'd get at a state park in the USA, running water, not hot. Outhouse toilets. I grew up poor and these are the sorts of camps my family vacationed at when I was a boy, so it was comfortable enough for me.

Figure 8. Rustic resort in Senegal viewed from lagoon approach.

We ate a simple dinner, fish and rice, and talked. I was not yet a coach, though when I look back on this trip, I see the seeds of that desire to encourage missionaries, later I discovered the methodology.

Phil was tired and went to bed. I was wired up on sugary "Chinese gunpowder" tea, and I went out to wander the sandbar alone.

You might think that I was in the middle of nowhere but I wasn't. (I experienced the middle of nowhere in Congo and New York City and on the Internet.) I wasn't in the middle of nowhere, but I *was* on the very edge of the world. There is a difference. In the middle of nowhere, you feel a lack of connection; it comes from our idea of what we experience in places like Congo: no peers, no connection with community, past or future, lapses in communication with home, and a place of disorienting limbo.

Our concept of it comes from literal hypo-connectivity but our typical experience of it now more frequently comes from the mirror opposite, that is, hyper-connectivity: so crowded, like a Manhattan street where in the midst of our frantic pace, we virtually disappear (and we end up hiring high dollar shrinks to stay sane).

For the remainder of this essay, "the middle of nowhere" refers to this hyper-connectivity that strangely mirrors that hypo-connectivity we originally took the phrase from. If you do not live in the middle of a huge city (New York, Bangkok, Mumbai), then it's possible that your middle of nowhere is usually your time spent on the Internet. In both the physical megacity and the virtual megalopolis, you lose perspective from the overwhelming hyper-connection. You do not say hello to that small-town grocer anymore, the one who knows you don't eat gluten. Instead, you merely enforce the shell around your bubble, making sure that your own space is secure. As you become immune to a friendly smile by never letting down your guard, you lose perspective on where to find civility.

But the way I define *on the edge of the world*, you sense the surface tension, your spirit acknowledges connection with the place where air and water collide, you feel that you can touch the atmospheric bubble that separates breathable air from the void of space. On the edge of the world, you are hyper-aware of your connections to earth, sea, sky and the fire of spirit, and to people—that is, when someone happens along your beach, you can smile and wave, you can see if they need a drink of water (you can see their individuality); if they do, you can give them one in the name of Jesus because you have seen them the way He does. This is a place where you can admit that you are completely naked before the Creator, and this edge of the world is not a place where we are ashamed of our vulnerability. When you stand on the brink of the void in this way, you find meaning in life; any humanity you encounter is met with authenticity of the experience. You are not over connected the way you are on the Internet. You are not under-connected, the way I was in the Congo.

That night in Senegal on the sandbar, there was not a cloud in the sky, and less light pollution than I've ever seen. The Atlantic Ocean stretched before me all the way to Brazil and the sky above was lit up with more stars than I had ever seen before; it stretched to eternity, and I was in right relationship with the Creator, naked as Adam, every hair counted.

The next morning over breakfast, Phil asked how I had enjoyed my late-night walk. I admitted that I wasn't on the dune long before I felt compelled to strip off my swim trunks and stand there in my birthday suit, sitting in awe before the eternity of stars, and vastness of the ocean—arguably the two most uninhabitable, unknowable and beautiful things ever created (created before man and outlasting us as individuals). You might have felt that no plants or creatures were yet created, sand, water and stars giving texture to the void, that you were in a time between the great void and the day of breath, you felt perhaps you had a glimpse of the second or third day of creation. Confronted with nature in such an original state, I worshipped God in my most original state.

Matching my confession, Phil said, "Yeah. I've done that here before, myself."

We admitted these things to each other somewhat shyly but with a mutual understanding: the edge of the known world where the surface tension becomes palpable and the fish can breathe air, elephants can swim diving deep, the naked are clothed, the mute are heard, the stars are known by name, the ocean touches the sky at the horizon, and we can see ourselves clearly for whom we are. We are not alone as we are in the middle of nowhere, walking through a city of people who guard their smiles like the Queen's Guard at Buckingham Palace; surfing the vast web soon to host 6 billion of us in terrifying anonymity each of us asserting our basic goodness. At the edge of the world, we know our logic is faulty, our bodies made mostly of water are even now breaking down, yet we embrace the cosmos.

Taleb is right: our advances in technology outpace our own ability to comprehend it so that every moment we spend with such technology thrusts us more and more into the middle of nowhere.[28] We lose perspective every moment that we spend with our technology, our worldview narrowing to an illusion of connectivity which is really a veneer covering our deepening, essential lost-ness. This loss of perspective makes it harder and harder to listen to our environment.

A strategy for great listeners must include a regular journey to the edge of the known world, a place where we shed our trappings and find our original state, a perspective on our smallness, and then just listen to the heartbeat of the universe, to God. This is not to say that we will then begin to be able to predict the future, but we should be able to at least judge the seasonal shifting better, the way the Canada goose and the monarch butterfly can do; all the migratory animals. The wildebeest herds which smell water and move collectively towards it, the pods of whales who mysteriously but intelligently telegraph their direction as they travel thousands of miles for reasons still unknown.

A great listener's job is not to predict the future but it is to provide that perspective beyond the comfortable (technologically controlled, air-conditioned, jet-speed transported) so that people can have a sense of the even bigger picture and make decisions that are in tune with a broader world than they normally perceive. In other words, we invite people to go to the edge of the world and connect.

❖ Where is the edge of your known world, and what do you get from connecting at that edge? How often do you go there? Write a plan to get there again.

❖ What activity puts you in danger of getting lost in the middle of nowhere?

Article 15

Dreaming

Your old men shall dream dreams,
and your young men shall see visions.
—Joel 2:28

I asked an older client whose coaching goals center around his legacy planning, who was the youngest member of his team. That youngest man is 31; 41 years younger. So I asked, what do you dream of for this organization 40 years from now? What will it look like when this younger man is your age? Then I told him perhaps he will be there to see it. We agreed that there is a good chance that he could make 30 more years, but a pretty slim chance for 40.

It's amazing that we Americans do not usually think in such broad terms. Many of us get so busy we've forgotten to make a six-month plan (it happens to me!).

For a time, I tried to sell solar panels. It was a disaster. Nobody's interested in something that will pay for itself in 15 years. But in other parts of the world, it's not uncommon for people to buy property that will pay for itself in 100 years. Europe is kicking the USA's rear end in renewable energy because they're much more used to thinking about their estates in the long term. The payoff isn't quick enough to spend the money on it. I was often told, with the additional reasoning that northern Indiana doesn't generate enough with photovoltaic cells to make a dent.

Northern Indiana can generate 4.5 kilowatt hours per square foot. Germany, at its southernmost point roughly 400 miles closer to the North Pole, has installed more solar capacity than any other country. The Germans obviously disagree with my neighbors! The key is a particular perspective on reality: large swaths of the American public's consciousness simply doesn't believe that climate change is a reality. It's hard to make sweeping reform unless it's predicated on a different vision of the future based on a sense that things aren't OK as they are now. The solution isn't immediate. Sometimes the solution isn't even a plan, it's just a direction. Get this: "The German revolution has come from the grass roots: Individual citizens and energy *genossenshcaften*—local citizens associations—have made half the investment in renewables." [29]

And to be sure, a 40-year vision is not always a completed plan. It's a dream, a direction. It's an invitation to talk less about the tools or technology the organization is now using (if it changes as much in the next 40 years as it has since 1975, it's completely inconceivable) and to focus more on the values that attracted this man to the ministry of this non-profit in 1975 and will still attract people in 2055 to engage the ministry of this particular organization, regardless of what tools it uses.

We like our lifetime warranties in the States, but we rarely think much about what will come beyond. Legacy planning should start before you're 70! What we are building is a question we can even begin in our 20s and 30s if we dare. Ask a young man what a particular organization will be in 150 years, and an old man what it will be in 40. It gives us direction and focus to think beyond the lifetime warranty. When we create products this way, we don't need to hang a lifetime warranty on them! People will see our earnestness. Ask people how their vision extends beyond their lifetime.

I've been leading an organization for 12 months now. I'm already thinking about how to prepare for handing it off to the next leader in seven to ten years. The organization will outpace my ability to lead it. I'll bring the entrepreneur's approach. One day, it will need the focused guidance of a manager. That energizes me to think beyond my own usefulness. When I asked my friend who is 71 to envision 40 years out, you might think he'd be discouraged to think about his own imminent death, but instead it gave him energy to finish his work well.

The interesting thing to me about the verse that says your old men will dream dreams, and young men will see visions, is that this is an inverted position; a paradigm that turns the world on its head. Typically, young men are dreamers and the old men have the ability to see visions. But to ask a young man for a vision, or an old man for a dream, is literary foregrounding, it jolts people out of their usual way of thinking. Either way, we ask that they look for something bigger than themselves. It will always motivate!

❖ If you are young (under 45), what vision do you hope for? How will the world be different in 150 years if you pursue it today?

❖ If you are old (over 45), what dream do you have for the era just after you die? If you would live to 105 years old, what do you dream of for the following decade?

Article 16

Invoking George Gobel

George Gobel was the greatest listener I ever met. I mean he could motivate dozens of people a day with just one simple, powerful question. He'd listen for hours at a time without saying a word, and when you walked away, you felt you could conquer the world. Five businessmen I knew personally became billionaires because of George Gobel. One of them sold more ice to the residents of Iceland than anybody could even imagine. George went to Chicago and sat in a meeting with the Chicago Cub's management team and the next year, they won the World Series. One time, the president asked him to come and sit in on a cabinet meeting. A few days later, Congress had a balanced budget and began paying off the national debt. He used to go hang out with the Dalai Lama and the Pope, both of whom would walk away with new insights.

When I was a kid, like most kids, I asked a ton of questions. Google didn't exist, so it wasn't uncommon for me to ask my dad questions he couldn't answer. So he'd just tell me, "George Gobel" and smile. Other times, though, I think he did know the answer but wanted me to figure it out myself. So he'd just say, "Ask George Gobel." Either way, I didn't get easy answers.

For quite a few years, I didn't believe that George Gobel existed—that he had ever been a real person. (Remember, Google didn't exist.) George Gobel was the ultimate authority on everything, had done everything, invented everything, and won every prize. George Gobel was my first Google—a repository of knowledge, a wealth of information, an infinite reference source. It's amazing I learned anything.

Dad's other tactic was to make up an answer. Perhaps he'd start with something that sounded plausible (based on an educated guess) but eventually he'd elaborate until he threw in a detail that was obviously turning his explanation into a tall tale. Eventually you'd figure out he was pulling your leg. "No, Dad! That's not true!" Then he'd laugh. He might say, "Well, if you don't believe me, maybe you should ask George Gobel!"

You'd almost think my Dad knew nothing.

"Dad, who discovered penicillin?"

George Gobel.

"Dad, who wrote the James Bond series?"

George Gobel.

"Dad, what's the name of that lady, that figure skater who won Olympic gold in 1968?"

Oh, that was George Gobel's sister, Georgette Gobel.

Rather than stifling my curiosity, getting an answer with *George Gobel* in it stimulated it. It took me a long time to find out what *pad Thai* was. I heard about these wonderful noodles in a pop song reference in about 1989, a solid five years before the Internet. Dictionaries didn't list it. It wasn't in the encyclopedia. But I never stopped seeking the answer.

As you become a better motivator and listener, even those who know that our listening skills, not our advice, are the strongest reason to talk with us, will still ask for advice from time to time.

That is the time to invoke George Gobel.

I have not done this with coaching clients, but it's wonderful with children. Last night at the dinner table my four-year-old daughter was having trouble figuring out which of the six people at the table didn't have a sister (it was her). I whispered to her. *It's George Gobel!* Instant giggles.

In our family's odyssey, George Gobel represented all mystery and was the explanation for all knowledge that could be craved. The wilder the claim, the more likely Gobel would get the credit. We began by taking the answer "George Gobel" to mean that Dad *didn't know,* which eventually allowed him to use the same answer to disguise the fact that he *did know!*

That's where it really becomes valuable.

Now here's where I let you down. In reality, Gobel was a comedian, best known for the George Gobel Show, a weekly program on NBC which ran from 1954–1960. (Don't you feel somehow poorer for knowing this already? The facts of his life make him much less interesting than the patina my dad painted upon his own memory of the man.)

Figure 9. George Gobel with his co-star Phyllis Avery who played his wife, Alice, on the George Gobel Show, 1959.

What does all this silliness have to do with motivational listening? The motivational listener intentionally does not know the answer and may even give an answer that inspires curiosity, mystery, and further investigation.

Not knowing the answer, in other words, is far more powerful than knowing the answer. Knowing the answer is a dangerous position to be in if you're motivating. Curiosity on the others' part, when you're listening, is one of their most powerful motivators, an ally for you. Dispelling curiosity with a straight answer concludes the matter most abruptly. Instead, referring to an epic figure like George Gobel may appear on the surface to be a flippant and evasive posture. But if anything is knowable, the best thing children, coaching clients, and co-workers who are talking to you can receive from you is an invitation to find out for themselves; to be redirected to George Gobel.

❖ Where do you apply tall tales or invoke mythical figures?

❖ What does it do for those you motivate?

❖ How does it help them think bigger?

Article 17

Playing the "good guy"

Someone once walked up to Jesus and said, "Ahem, uh, excuse me, good Teacher–"

Jesus interrupted him. "Why do you call me good? No one is good but God alone."[30]

Jesus already knew the guy was looking for a little justification. Okay, maybe a lot. *But I'm pretty much a good guy, right? I get to keep and protect what's mine, right?* But if you call Jesus good (and therefore call him God and Master), it's time to recognize your essential badness and lay down your weapons against your neighbors. His example was not one of self-defense; instead, he surrendered His own life.

The problem raised by expanding possibilities within the realm of imagination and expanding truth is that we must learn to judge situations differently. We usually react to an affront by contracting somehow, rolling our fist tightly into a ball, for example. Instead, when we listen, we want to learn to recognize that we may not be the good guy right now, and lay down our lives. (Jesus, of course, was the good guy, but He accepted the role of bad guy willingly).

When I was a kid, we used to play "cops and robbers" or the now-less-politically-correct "cowboys and Indians" which games were entirely constructed around the idea that we would now spend an hour pretending to shoot each other dead and arguing about who hit or missed whom. Usually the kid who had to be the "bad guy" didn't really like his role. It was always the kid on the low end of the pecking order, wasn't it? Hunted like a fox, he'd hide and retreat, getting "shot" repeatedly and being told he's dead many times over, while he insisted, "No, I hit you first, you missed me," to all the rest of us: his pursuers, vigilantes of righteousness, dispensers of justice, or, when seen from the other side of the neutral zone, fascist bullies. None of us wants to be the guy who takes the hit.

This is the problem. In our imaginations, we are always the good guy. In reality, we cannot be so sure.

But by now, most of us have figured out that maybe the cowboys weren't really the "good guys" in the "cowboys and Indians" scenario. In my town, in spite of a vocal contingency fighting to retain the moniker "Redskins" for the high school's mascot, the school board voted for a name change 5–2. This is 2015. We've known that *redskin* is an offensive term for a long time now. We're finally changing. And you know what's most remarkable? After the school board voted to make the change, the Pokagon Band of Potawatomi offered to pay the entire bill for all signage change, an estimated $16,000. That's graciousness in action.

If you ever played Robin Hood, you knew that suddenly the cops were the bad guys. How did that happen? All along, even as children, we are aware that most police officers have the best in mind for us—we know that if we are lost we can look for a man or woman in uniform and find help, but we also know that corruption happens in Merrie Olde England, in Congo, and all too often in Chicago as well. As children, we are aware that not one of us is good.

What about the United States armed forces? Aren't they the good guys? Our soldiers themselves know that the waters have

become very murky. Ask them when they come home. They
know:

"[The United States Armed Forces] does not
exist to give you money for school. The organization exists to assert the political will of the United
States government against other people by force
of arms. And what they do is not like it's portrayed in the movies. They're not sending you out
there to be a hero, they're sending you out there
to be a bullet... it's never been about that. The fact
that some people fight back and put you in danger is also part of the equation, but . . . Why, why .
. . why put yourself in a position to go over there
and be forced by a circumstance not of your
choosing to take the life of another human being
who's a total stranger? Because they're not some
evil caricature like you've seen in films and all
that stuff. They're people. They have mothers,
they have fathers, they have sisters, they have
brothers, they have children. There's people that
love them just like there's people that love you.
And those people grieve, when they lose them,
just like people grieve if they lose you. That's
maybe not as dramatic and exciting and clear-cut
and easy to understand; this sort of simple binary
world of good and evil that you get painted for
you, but that's not the way the real world is. And
in the real world you have to live with the conse-
quences of your decisions the rest of your life.
Think hard. I served in eight conflict areas, and I
raised my hand ... five times during the course of

my career, and took an oath, and that oath was to protect and defend the Constitution of the United States from all enemies, foreign and domestic, and I went to eight conflict areas. I never met a single person who was an enemy of the United States Constitution. Not one. There are no enemies of the Constitution. I did spend a lot of time going out there, again, and becoming a political instrument for trans-national corporations and to preserve American military and political supremacy around the world, but that's not in the oath! That's not in the oath. There's nobody threatening the constitution in Vietnam, there's nobody threatening the constitution in Grenada, Guatemala, El Salvador, Columbia, Peru, Somalia, Haiti—I went to all those places, I never met anybody that was a threat to the constitution, or the principles of the Constitution for that matter; I just met people, and they put me in circumstances where I had to do a lot of things I wish I didn't have in my head right now."[31]

—Retired Special Forces Master Sargent Stan Goff

I never served in a branch of the United States Armed Forces, but I applaud this solider. Along the way, he learned to listen, to observe the truth of what was going on around him. He heard what people were against, and what they weren't.

In March of 1997, at age 23, I stood on a street corner in Abidjan, Ivory Coast. A transport truck full of American infantry went past. They were either on their way to or returning from Liberia, where they joined U.N. Forces ensuring the cease-fire since August of '96, after seven years of civil war, which resulted in the election of Charles Taylor four months later. (He turned out to be a real winner: Taylor is serving 50 years after being found guilty on all 11 counts of aiding and abetting war crimes and crimes against humanity, a verdict he was given at The Hague in 2012).

I looked at my khakis, threadbare after three months of being washed by my Ivoirian "mothers"—that is, washed by hand, by Africans in whose homes I had boarded, whose food I had shared.

I remember thinking to myself that the soldiers in the truck, most of whom were probably about my age, were getting a very different picture of Africa than I was. There were some similarities, to be sure. They probably went home feeling they hadn't really done much, as did I. But there were differences. A major difference here, as I reflected later on a sermon given by Laura Oyer at Thrive one Sunday in October, 2015, is that there is a difference between peacekeepers and peacemakers. The soldiers in the trucks were headed to Liberia as peacekeepers. When they left, Charles Taylor took over, and with his seizure of power, peace went out the window. I could only hope that some would be able to come home with reflections like Stan Goff's. Probably they didn't do anything bad, perhaps for the span of the ceasefire, they did something good. As for myself, living with the people of Ivory Coast was the work of a peacemaker. Think of it this way: A referee stands on the outside, keeps the peace. A good coach sits on the bench with the team. The coach makes peace.

Quite reasonably, my editor cautioned me here. There are moments when we are attacked by insane organisms or organizations (those who really are an "enemy of the Constitution"). It's not about Iraq or any specific place. In the philosophical world of pacifism, the Nazi party in Germany or today's ISIS may be special cases, but I'm not addressing that hairy issue. I'm staying focused on a philosophy of listening that means I will be the first to lay down my weapons (and words are weapons too).

I'm addressing us. The philosophy I'm espousing here is about my personal responsibility and intention to take a non-violent posture to improve my listening. The people I listen to *must* know that I will not strike out against them. Coaching athletes who think you'll strike out against them at any moment may win a title or two as Bob Knight was able to do. But the coaching work of those who follow principles of motivational listening are much more likely to build trust, and win over the long term. The minute a violent response becomes a possibility, the conversation has already ended. This goes for international diplomacy, but it also goes for interpersonal relationships. The minute your employee thinks you might fire them, you're working uphill.

Two guys in Ionia, Michigan, both of whom had concealed-carry permits and were legally packing heat, had an incident of road rage. According to an article by Angie Jackson, September 20, 2013:

> "The mother of Jim Pullum, who was killed in an apparent road rage encounter, claims Robert Taylor came out shooting after her son pulled into an Ionia car wash....
>
> "'He shot at Jim first, then he shot Jim again while Jim was reaching in his car to get his gun....'
>
> "[Jim Pullum then shot Robert Taylor and both died.] Investigators have not confirmed Bernadine Pullum's account of the encounter. Taylor's family did not respond to interview requests. Bill King, Taylor's next door neighbor in

Ionia, described him as friendly and a 'good guy.'"[32]

Wait a minute. Wasn't Robert Taylor the one who shot first? Angie Jackson's follow-up article on November 2 indicates that the two exchanged words, including the fact that Pullum said a vehicle behind him "needed to get off his ass" before Taylor opened fire.[33]

Most stories about incidents like this will include someone like a neighbor, saying, "But he was a 'good guy.'" So which one was the good guy, Pullum or Taylor? Why are we so surprised when two good guys kill each other? None of us are "good."

I'm continually aghast at how people try to figure out who is the good guy in a situation when it comes to the use of weapons. When picking teams or who's-it, instead of "eenie-meenie-miney-mo" or "engine, engine number 9" we might have had a mantra like this:

"Concealed-carry, military, curley-moe-and-larry, dirty harry. Good guys are good—and / bad / guys /are / ... it." And you better be running if you're the bad guy.

The fundamental human problem with carrying weapons to protect ourselves against the bad guys is that none of us are the good guy. Not one of us.

What if we changed the name of every hospital or clinic now called "The Good Samaritan" and contemporized the title of these institutions to "The Good Palestinian"? How would it change our perspective on the old question, "Who is my neighbor?"[34]

(Christians argue with me, but Palestinians are terrorists! and I reply, yes, it's true, and some Palestinians are Christians, too. Nobody calls them Samaritans anymore, but that is their heritage, so I think the name fits.)

Expanding the possibilities of who might be our neighbor means discovering that we are not so much the good guy as we thought.

What makes this a critical issue for motivational listening? The fact that people will make horrible mistakes, escalating conflict, and resulting in death is *not* an outlier. They seem like surprises, because we thought people were "good guys" but we do well to stay grounded in this reality even as we expand the possibilities of truths hoped for—that we would do well to remember, so that we don't give up. The incident of road rage and the situations Stan Goff experienced while "defending the Constitution" are not surprises. They're tragically common. We envision a better future in spite of these things, and we don't quit or give up when people fail. As I established earlier, we know that most will not be great, but now we know that *none* will be good.

* Where are you tempted to consider yourself the "good guy"?

* What will it take to walk away from that security?

* How will giving up your own security impact how you listen to others?

* Where can you give up your right to defend yourself verbally?

Article 18

Listening, violence and good news

Pilate asked Jesus, "What is truth?"[35] Pilate was trolling Jesus. Pilate had seen enough in his political career to recognize that truth was whatever the most powerful person said it was. Caesar says he's a god? OK, fine, he's a god, who is arguing with that? After all, Caesar can decide if you live or die, even if you rank as high as Pilate did, and that's pretty darn close, practically speaking, to being a god.

Pilate was a pragmatist in an extremely impractical situation. No wonder he tried trolling. "Truth" was a bait word. Jesus, however, had been trolled by the best of them (the Pharisees) and knew that He'd said all He wanted to say publicly, and wasn't interested in discussions of truth (absolute Truth with a capital T or otherwise, for example, the facts of His case, or the expanding possibilities He was in the process of enacting) when the asker wasn't really interested. Truth is not worth discussing with a mostly disinterested relativist. They will concede you're right when they feel like it, or argue if they feel ornery. In this case, Pilate wasn't really interested in a discussion, anyway. Like a good executive does, he'd recognized his most likely course of action pretty quickly and the rest was just a search for a decent Plan B. Or perhaps just a good rationalization for Plan A.

A motivational listener doesn't waste time in discussions where the speaker isn't interested in self-discovery of the truth. A speaker has to have his own ears open for the conversation to be of any value.

So, Jesus chose instead not to defend Himself. I've previously stated my concern about our addiction to being the "good guy" and I think that oftentimes our eagerness to defend ourselves comes from this cultural attitude that "I am a pretty good guy."

The same thing happens when we argue with a co-worker, spouse or other family member, or a member of our church. Even worse, when we're doing it publicly on the Internet hiding behind an avatar or screen name. Why do we defend our position? Because we feel threatened somehow. A threat to our way of life. A threat to our environment. A threat to our body or wallet.

When Jesus was arrested, Peter certainly felt threatened, so he lashed out.[36] But when Peter cut off Malchus's ear, it wasn't an accident. Think of how unlikely it is that the wild, untrained flailing of Peter's sword would connect with only the earlobe— not the shoulder, neck, nor any other part of the head of the servant. The more I think about this, I'm convinced it was no accident. The ear is an object lesson. When we defend ourselves violently, we damage the other person's ability to hear anything. We may have good news to share with them later, and without an ear, they can't exactly hear it. This is the last time we see Jesus performing a healing miracle during His earthly life. How did we come up with the servant's name? He was just a servant, right? I mean, lots of slaves are mentioned in the Bible without a name. In this case, Malchus isn't just a slave. He's a person. Somewhere along the line, the writer of the gospel of John made sure to find out Malchus's name.

After Jesus said, "Put away your sword," there is no histori-cally recorded example of Christians using violence until the time of Constantine. I believe that the early Christians understood "put away your sword" to be a permanent injunction, because the mission of a drawn sword is in direct conflict with the mis-sion to share good news. News given at sword-point is never good news.

The use of violent weapons by nation states, whether in the name of religion or not, ensures that they and their enemies will no longer hear each other. No other argument for pacifism at a personal or national level is necessary for those who carry a vi-sion for the kingdom coming on earth as it is in heaven and who carry a mission of sharing this good news as a now-and-coming reality.

Do you want to be heard, or not? Do you want people to be able to hear? We can't motivate if we aren't heard, or if we can't be heard because of previous violence.

Motivational listening is done in the context and presence of peace.

❖ Where do you find peace in the midst of an accusatory world?

❖ Where have you been tempted to lash out like Peter did? What does it mean to you to put away your sword so that people like Malchus can keep their ears?

Article 19

TED Listening

The vocational listener may choose to eschew public speaking engagements. Talking about listening is like a baseball pitcher telling you how to catch. The listener demonstrates listening by listening.

(Training is different than speaking. Typically as a coach trainer, I still end up spending more than 50 percent of my time listening. I'm on the platform, but it's not about my ideas.)

The popular secular version of preaching are TED and TEDx Talks.

But what would it look like to do TED (Technology, Entertainment, Design) Listening? The TED listener would bring an audience member up on stage. The audience member, a former nobody, becomes the expert speaker—they're an expert on their own life. The TED listener hears their expertise and spotlights the brilliance the audience member-become-expert didn't even know they contained. In awe, the audience begins to realize that they, too, may be an expert, and may have something to contribute to society. Then, of course, everyone watches it on YouTube.

❖ Where do you have the guts to ask somebody to talk to your own audience without censoring it or knowing how it's going to make you look beforehand?

Article 20

Surface tension

Surface tension is the elasticity that allows a liquid to attain the least amount of surface area possible. The water strider (when I was a kid we called them water "skeeters") walks on water and the surface tension is his ally.

If you want to walk on water, you must make that surface tension between the physical world and spiritual world your ally, not your enemy.

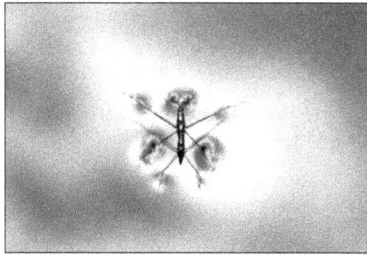

Figure 10. Water strider or "skeeter" a,k.a. Gerridae.

When you say, "Will this idea float?" you are not asking to set down pylons of concrete to support it, you are looking, listening for a positive reaction to the surface tension: buoyancy. You are recognizing the water and the air together—how they meet to create a special zone where the mass and volume work, where the conditions are just right, where, at the edge of your known world, you can sail forward.

The time it takes to listen well also takes elasticity. In fact, for people trying out an idea for the first time, it requires the same sort of encouragement as I used to get from Dad when I wanted to jump off the diving board.

"You'll float," he'd say, "*and* I'll catch you."

One of my favorite ways to ask powerful questions has to do with, "What have you not even spoken out loud yet? What idea do you have, what dream?"

The comedian David Letterman had a segment on his show called "Will it Float?" Part of the shtick was that David always asserted, no matter what item was announced, "It'll float." Sometimes he'd second-guess himself, but his first reaction was always positive. A glass brick? A box of taffy? A massage machine? A cheese log? He always said, "I think it'll float!"

That's the attitude, Dave. We have to start with the assumption that *something* will float.

❖ Where in your life are you willing to say "this will float" even if Jesus seems to be asleep?

Article 21

When nothing exciting is happening

Sometimes our only job is to float, particularly when we've wrecked. Preparation for listening for significance is in our approach to mundane existence. By mathematical default, the ten most extraordinary moments of self-discovery in our lives are surrounded by millions of less-extraordinary moments, just as a wrecked ship is surrounded by millions of acres of ordinary ocean.

So the mundane must be seen as the essential framework or container with which we uphold the extraordinary, to keep it from scraping bottom.

Imagine a buoy on the ocean, perhaps an extraordinary thing to find when you're adrift, perhaps a sign pointing you towards home. Imagine finding that buoy without the ocean itself supporting it. The molecules which sit atop the ocean create surface tension, and so, at the edge of the world, you find that you can float. We float on the mundane, we are buoyed ourselves by surface tension.

So the mundane is the ocean, and the extraordinary moment of self-discovery or aid is the buoy. It's only noticeable when you're looking carefully at the mundane for signs of something other.

The motivational listener isn't bored with the mundane, she is fascinated by its potential to support something extraordinary and examines it expectantly for signs of a surprise.

Pay the price of embracing the mundane if you want to find the extraordinary. Recently, I dropped in at my friend Charles' office. Charles knew that I'd had several coaching sessions that morning.

He asked, "How did your coaching sessions go?" and I responded, "Nothing amazing, but my clients are happy and progressing with their projects."

I think that when we watch someone really listen for the first time and the person who is talking becomes more and more animated, finally having a transformational breakthrough—that is when we start to believe that listening always needs to be somehow amazing. Most of the listening I do happens when people are working on mundane stuff. But I'm always scanning the horizon for an extraordinary moment, a Black Swan event. Keep your eyes peeled!

❖ What mundane relationships in your life are worth your attentiveness, even if they remain static?

❖ What relationships don't provide drama or require intensive attention? What's good about that?

❖ What glimpses of the exceptional have you had within those relationships, and how often?

❖ Who do you value for their steadiness?

❖ What do you hope for each of these people even as you accept their relative mundane-ness, stability, static-ness, or durability?

Article 22

Alert scientists travel internationally, deliver housewarming gifts

O
n June 30, 2015, Jupiter and Venus came closer to each other than they'd ever been since the years BC 3–2 in an event called a *conjunction*. They were one-third of a degree apart, and to the naked eye looked like one very bright star or one very small moon. Brighter than anything else in the sky. You didn't need a telescope to see it. My wife and some of our kids went out and looked and there it was. These two planets, what ancient astronomers and astrologers thought of as "wandering stars" (because they did not stay within a constellation's formation like other stars) are thought to be the same two "stars" which came together as the "Star of Bethlehem."

The Magi of the East studied the mundane movements of stars and gradually made associations like "King" for Jupiter and "Love or Birth" for Venus, expecting that one day the gods or God would show them something worth following up on, worthy enough to respond with significant action such as international travel and expensive housewarming gifts. The reward for their continual alertness to the mundane movements of the planets was a singular moment in history, a surprise like no other.

Science is about repetitive observation where one methodically records experiments and results over and over. But there's an art to taking the discoveries from many years, even hundreds or thousands of years of observation, and interpreting it correctly.

Scientists, I suppose, would have trouble accepting a redneck's story of an unidentified flying object sighting (or shepherds who say that angels sang to them).

People observe the signs of different phenomena in different ways, and this isn't about which way is right or wrong. The point is that you have to keep your eyes open, then you have to be willing to believe exactly what you're seeing.

When I saw Jupiter and Venus dancing together on June 30, 2015, I had a new understanding of just how powerful this must have been for the scientists in Persia in 3 BC. In perhaps hundreds of years of observation (during which time they somehow connected one planet with *kingship* and the other with *birth*), they had never seen these two so close. But what did I do? I looked at it for a while, tried to take some pictures with sadly inadequate equipment, then I went back inside where I probably did something like check my email or say goodnight to my daughter. The scientists stared until the stars sank in the western sky—precisely in the direction of Jerusalem. Which way to go? To check your email now, or go toward Jerusalem?

The motivational listener must stay alert and focused during the mundane moments of life. You're looking for signs, and you don't get too many chances to see the big ones, but you only know the unusual by first knowing the usual.

❖ What or who is worth monitoring just in case something big happens?

❖ How will you keep tabs on it/them?

Article 23

Sonder

Sonder is the realization that each random passerby has a life as vivid and complex as your own.

From John Koenig's web series:

"You are the main character—the protagonist—the star at the center of your own unfolding story. You're surrounded by your supporting cast: friends and family hanging in your immediate orbit. Scattered a little further out, a network of acquaintances who drift in and out of contact over the years.

"But there in the background, faint and out of focus, are the extras. The random passersby. Each living a life as vivid and complex as your own. They carry on invisibly around you, bearing the accumulated weight of their own ambitions, friends, routines, mistakes, worries, triumphs and inherited craziness. When your life moves on to the next scene, theirs flickers in place, wrapped in a cloud of backstory and inside jokes and characters strung together with countless other stories you'll never be able to see. That you'll never know exists.

"In which you might appear only once. As an extra sipping coffee in the background. As a blur of traffic passing on the highway. As a lighted window at dusk."[37]

I discovered Koenig's work just as I was writing on the importance of seeking and celebrating peoples' complexity when we're engaged in motivational listening. Koenig coins words to give definition to emotions or epiphanies for which we don't yet have a word; this was a word I needed in my lexicon!

Sonder was the first word on the list of Koenig's creations that someone posted to Facebook. Since it relates directly to what I've been working on all day, I decided to pluck it off the virtual shelf and out of the artist's neo-dictionary and discuss it some more.

First of all, I don't think we ever can fully realize sonder. We may realize it in little epiphanies while we eavesdrop or people-watch. We may very intentionally seek to engage sonder as we listen. We do have to slow down from our own spinning along our merry way, and get off the merry-go-round of our life, long enough to recognize that someone else has an orbit too.

It occurs to me that perhaps Galileo discovered it first. He pointed out that our earth is not the center of the universe, and this was a dangerous thing partly because it contrasted directly with the poetic biblical proofs which indicated he was a heretic. Beyond the proof of the earth being the center of the galaxy as evidenced in Scripture's infallible poetry, there was a lack of sonder in general.

Galileo must have looked about himself and seen that people were not willing to give up the idea that their own orbit was more vivid or complex than his was, and so, without sonder, they couldn't grasp how Galileo could even exist. Galileo, as a vivid and complex person, became invisible behind what he represented, and the only alternative left once we've shrouded someone behind our lack of sonder is that we would destroy them to maintain our illusion.

What we're looking for in ourselves as we engage the concept of motivational listening is sonder. We try to step away from our concern over our own spinning planet, to jump off that merry-go-round and immerse ourselves in the others' complexity for a while. There was a time when I was supposed to be listening to someone and my wife was crying about a family situation in the next room. I was distracted from my client's orbit by that of my wife—an orbit much more closely tied to my own. But when we really focus, we find that they know their world exquisitely, their life, which we see in black and white, is in vivid color for them. We do remain an outside observer—but an engaged one who is thinking less about our own issues than we are about theirs, at least for a while. We sacrifice something to engage our sonder. Instead of destroying or shrouding their world, we enter into it for all we are worth, seeking to celebrate their vividity and complexity.

Of course, Galileo was not the first to recognize sonder. He only lived in a time when the recognition of sonder was a rare commodity. The first Adam recognized suddenly his nakedness, meaning that he suddenly discovered not only that he was not the center of the universe, but that others might see him not being the center of the universe and laugh to think that he'd once lacked any awareness that he wasn't the center of the universe. At the same moment, he realized that Eve had a life as vivid and complex as his own. That's scary enough to make you want to put on an extra layer of clothing.

The second Adam, the Son of Man, Jesus was full of sonder, so full that in His vision for each of us to have a fully vivid and complex life, so that we could enter into an orbit around Him forever, He would be a willing supernova. Naked. On a cross. For the sake of our vivid complexity.

In O'Hare Airport on my way to Congo in September of 2015, a man sat down next to me, turned the other direction and politely asked a woman to take a picture of him with his cell phone while he put on one of those little sleeping masks over his eyes and pretended to doze in one of those uncomfortable airport chairs. She agreed.

I turned to the two of them and said, "I really wanted to photobomb that picture!" The man said, "Yes! That would be hilarious!" So we took another photo, the man "sleeping" again (though unable to contain a smile) this time with me in the background, giving the camera a thumbs up. A woman sitting behind him heard the conversation and joined in for the fun of a photobomb too. Four complete strangers, one with a mask, one with the masked man's cell phone, and two random passers-by, all recognizing the humor and experiencing a lighthearted moment of sonder

Figure 11. Photo provided via text by random but friendly stranger.

together, the joy of interacting with strangers who would then go on with their lives, with perhaps just a sliver of additional hope for humanity based on a tiny but pleasant interaction. I even had the guy text me the photo. We wished each other pleasant travels. None of them could have guessed the photo would end up in my book, but that's the point of sonder, you just don't know what impact your passing by will make.

❖ What can you do to wish other travelers a pleasant journey?

Article 24

The anointed listener

One of my original concepts for the book on motivational listening was a discussion of the anointed listener because I wanted to contrast it with the idea of an anointed speaker which is the religious version of a motivational speaker. Though there's a lot of religious references in the book, I wanted to appeal to a broader audience. So, while a lot of my articles have really been broader than just Christian-faith-and-church-work scenarios, I'm returning to my original concept of the "anointed listener" for this article.

Religious tourism has been around a long time. The Ganges River with 20 million visitors annually and Mecca with 13 million are the biggest destinations for religious tourism.[38] Since the Middle Ages, Christians (or anybody who was on a quest for meaning) could journey through the Pyrenees across southern France all the way to western Spain on El Camino de Santiago, a pilgrimage still walked by thousands today. Of course, the Middle Ages also brought us the Crusades.

Go on Crusade, come home with a piece of the cross or perhaps a sacred relic from a Saint, a bone spur, perhaps in a small exotic box—something that these days you might see on eBay selling for thousands of dollars. A potato chip shaped like the Virgin Mary. Trekking, acquiring, returning, your life would never be the same. Or, you'd die in the process, which considering what it's like to be a serf, might not be so bad. Nobody really wants to admit they are a serf. As "Woman" in Monty Python's *Holy Grail* so aptly put it: "I didn't know we had a king. I thought we were an autonomous collective."

Anachronistic Marxist language aside, there's a broad appeal to not grubbing in the dirt all our lives I think we inherently understand. The grass is always greener on the other side of the fence, so it's attractive to go on a pilgrimage or short-term trip to visit an orphanage, help build a church, etc. Service seems like a great way to use vacation time in a wholesome way, educate students to a broader worldview, and at least pay lip service to "The Great Commission." Of course, that last phrase belies some of my cynicism. In recent times, short-term mission trips have come under fire. Some critical thinking about whether or not a foray into another culture without much orientation or training in how to do so sensitively is needed.

I'm not saying we should never go somewhere foreign to give something of ourselves, to be uncomfortable for the sake of others. After all, I'm only weeks away (as I rewrite this article) from a trip to Congo myself. I spent a year there 27 years ago. I have some cross-cultural training. I'm an intermediate French-language speaker, and in this case, I've been invited to lead training on a specific professional skill set I happen to have. I'm no expert on the Congo, but I think it's fair to say I'm a little more experienced cross-culturally than your average youth group member.

In spite of the fact that we may unleash upon an unsuspecting world some rather brash and insensitive North Americans and that we may do some damage to our reputation globally through short-term mission projects, there's no way we'll ever conquer our own myopic ethnocentrism if we never leave home. And we'll never develop savvy world travelers if we don't send people on their first trip. Some of them will say, "Icky! Bugs," and others will be fascinated, perhaps drawn to a longer-term vision. It used to be that you joined the mission movement, took your trunk aboard a steamer, and went. No training, no testing. Once you were dropped off, you lived or died in the jungle you chose. Now, there's room to explore without commitment. Like preparing for a marriage, you can fool around and stomp through the tulips sowing wild oats, or you can move cautiously, recognizing that you really don't know what you don't know, and listen to counsel and training before you make that long-term move. But you have to go on your first date before you know if you're in for life or not. In the U.S., we just don't do arranged marriages anymore, and we don't take that approach to service work either.

There is entertainment value in short term work. Not often enough do we cast vision for raising up long-term leadership before, during, or after those short-term trips. Sometimes, you're just going somewhere else. I love my hometown, but I really love to go somewhere else. I was comforted to learn from my friend, Michael Pollock, it's quite common for former missionary kids to consider airports their favorite place to be; it means you're in transition. When you grow up between cultures, transition is what you do best. I would almost always prefer to be *going* somewhere else. I have a problem with wanting to be somewhere else, and when other people get to go somewhere else, I feel jealous. Oh, I get wanderlust! So I understand why people like to do this stuff.

But here's the biggest problem: when you go somewhere else, you're out of context, unless you stay for seven years. SEVEN YEARS. By then, you're not somewhere else, you're just there. Of course, that means you're ready to get *going* again. Which is a problem too, because....

Real leadership and real impact happens here. Or there, after seven years. Even with my expertise, history, language skill, and professional knowledge, will an eight-day trip to Congo be deeply impacting? It's hard to say for sure that it will. (It may be deeply impacting for me, but I am not the point.)

These scenarios, going on short-term missions, going to conferences to hear powerful, anointed speakers, hoping for miraculous healing, entertained along the way, they all happen somewhere else. And that's very attractive and fun for us, and it truly does alter your worldview, at least for a while, and that has a LOT of value. We go because we will be impacted, not because we will have impact. The biggest impact we can hope for, however, happens when we listen *really carefully!*

Perhaps the biggest concern I have about religious tourism is that we might become (or create elsewhere) a bourgeoisie kingdom of God from waiting for the handout of bread and circuses from a mighty throne.

Charles Buller recently talked about his trek in Congo last March. He flew from Kinshasa to Kikwit, in southeast Congo. There, he and a Congolese pastor rode motorcycles 600 miles over six days back to Kinshasa. They visited churches that hadn't seen a (white) missionary in 20 years. "I'm sure some of them thought that this signaled the return of the missionary with all our money," he said. But that isn't going to happen in Congo. Their wait for a better Christian life economically sponsored by a western missionary is a pipe dream. The denominational mission-sending structures are weakened and mission just isn't being done the way Buller's parents did it. Short term or long term, the missionary movement is becoming economically inverted. People from poor countries are getting sent to wealthy ones.

So when we go, our *motivational listener mode* has to be on full-time alert. But our real impact is at home: somewhere we've invested for seven years or more.

The people who make the biggest impact on the Way of Santiago in Spain are not the pilgrims; they are the people who live each day along the route, giving generously to travelers. They see travelers in many states of being. I suspect mostly tired, but sometimes elated to reach a village, sometimes hungry, sometimes thirsty, sometimes wet and sometimes burned. The ones who live along the route are those who get to serve Christ daily as He said, "I was naked and you clothed me."[39] They sell food and lodging, of course, but they also reach out with encouragement and touch those who walk past without any way to know which ones are simply served and which ones will have their deepest moment of the entire pilgrimage because of their kindness. It seems like it would be easy to give kindness to a passing stranger on a daily basis when you live next to a pilgrimage route. I imagine that those people must be hyper-aware of sonder (see previous article).

I think the key to being an anointed listener is that we offer the opportunity for regular people, right here where we are (or perhaps *there*, once seven years has come and gone) to be the salt and light right now without having to go somewhere else. That's hard for me because I like to be on the move. I confess that I've said, "I'm coaching people in Germany, Bolivia, India and Alaska" with too much pride, but I'm less enthusiastic about the clients who live right here in Goshen, Indiana. To my friends in Goshen and Elkhart County, I'm sorry. I have been here for much more than seven years, very much on purpose, and I still miss that target and wish I were elsewhere, feeding on bourgeois bread and riding elephants in the circus. Thanks for sending me, each and every time you do send me. It's humbling to be invited, humbling to be sent, even more humbling to confess that I don't focus enough on the place I've chosen to invest long term.

Focusing on our own locality as a place to serve moves us from a lazy bourgeois mentality where we wait for things to come to us in the form of "anointed" entertainment from the outside or travel somewhere to get excited, healed, blessed or to be a blessing (bread and circuses) into a mobilized kingdom proletariat. The root of the word *proletariat* is "proles" meaning child-bearing. So, a mobilized proletariat is a kingdom of common workers who settle down and bear children. Bearing children is what we really want the common person in the kingdom to be about—and the greatest ones among us as well (because the last shall be first and vice versa). Bearing children is not ideal when you are on vacation. Women prefer to be settled. It's not that you can't do it when you're away from home, it just means you may end up rocking your baby to sleep in a manger.

Anointed speakers from abroad are a rarity, a luxury, a bath in rhetorical salts and oils, a balm, a cool breeze, and something we (those who attend revival meetings and go to hear travelling preachers) don't have to work very hard for. And it seems like they're usually somewhere else, so we either have to wait for them to come to us or we have to go to them. As the adage goes, an expert is someone who's more than 50 miles away, or as Jesus put it, "No prophet is acceptable in his own country." [40]

Anointed listeners should be here; or *there* after seven years; and everywhere. Marxist language of a proletariat, bourgeoisie, and silly autonomous collectives aside, the point is that anointed listening mobilizes a workforce, while the quest for religious experience *elsewhere* can breed complacency whenever we are at home—the place we ought least to be lazy. Anointed listening creates an atmosphere where the proletariat of the kingdom is empowered to BIRTH CHILDREN into the kingdom, and anointed speaking has the side danger of causing me, or inviting us, to expect that someone would do it for us, turn us on

somehow. That even anointed speaking would become entertainment, as the generations alive now in the twenty-first century are prone to desire.

> *With the lights out, it's less dangerous. Here we*
> *are now, entertain us.*
> *I feel stupid and contagious. Here we are now,*
> *entertain us.*
>
> —Nirvana

The world doesn't really need so many more anointed
speakers, anyway. "Let not many of you become teachers, my
brethren, for you know that we who teach shall be judged with
greater strictness."[41] But, the world does need more anointed
listeners: those who know how to tame their tongues, whether at
home or, when the time is right, abroad.

Some of my friends here in Goshen have half-jokingly suggested that the life coaching world is just a big MLM scam; you
get training so you can train others, so they can train others to
listen, but nobody ever makes a career out of it except the guy at
the top. Perhaps it is. It's certainly true that not many people
make a career out of it. I know many very good coaches who are
only part-timers. I'm starting to realize that though that's what I
happen to be called to, it's not really the point to make a career
out of it for most of us. The point is to mobilize a proletariat of
anointed listeners, here, there and everywhere, to birth children
for a kingdom unlike any this world has ever seen.

❖ What relationships have you invested in over seven years?

❖ What does that give you?

Where I be

If Dr. Seuss and J.R.R. Tolkien got together to write a pledge to become a better listener. Here is what they came up with:

> "I would listen in a box,
>   and I would listen to a fox.
> I could listen to a hobbit,
>   I will listen 'til you stop it.
> I would listen in a house,
>   and I would listen to a mouse.
> I will listen on the train,
>   and I will listen in the rain.
> I love to listen, Sam Gamgee,
>   I'm listening right where I be."

❖ You don't have to memorize this to pass the test.

Article 26

A dream of getting the
wax out of my ears
February 8, 2015

L ast night I had a dream, and the most important piece I remembered when I woke up was that in the dream someone cleaned a huge glob of wax out of my ear. My left ear.

For some reason, there were two nursing students, and then one said, "I can do it," and she bent over my head and reached in with a cotton swab or some sort of long probe and inserted it in my ear canal and out came the wax and we'll leave it at that. I hope this dream signifies something—a breakthrough. A breakthrough in how I listen, I hope.

Famed poet Billy Collins was reading a newer piece, titled *1956* on NPR[42] last night—his first verse talks about how the proverbial joke in jazz music is that a marriage counselor suggests to a couple who aren't communicating well that they ought to visit a jazz club because people always talk during a bass solo; but that the reality is this, as Collins puts it:

> "But of course no one starts talking just be-
> cause of a bass solo or any other solo for that
> matter. The quieter bass solo just reveals the

people in the club who have been talking all along."

Naked like Adam and Eve: revealed to be talking, laughing, flirting and drinking. Un-alert to the artistry happening around them. Sloppy in their boozy lust, or perhaps not even at the jazz concert with any expectation of engaging the music. I suppose it's not sloppy if you're not really an aesthete in the first place. It's just bad form, because you're there for the style of it, and you got found out—that you didn't have the class of a jazz aficionado, only a pretense of sophistication so you can score with some dame: I hope you remembered your fedora. So do you want to be a listener for the style of it (and therefore are going to get found out, recognized as a noise-maker even if only in your own head while you appear to be listening)? Or are you an aficionado and devotee to the jazz which is that life across the table from you? February 8, 2015 was my oldest son's twelfth birthday, a day on which I was nominated (by my almost-teenaged son, therefore, an honor) to take him and his two best friends to an entertainment venue an hour away, an expensive indoor gym with trampolines, $45 for three prepubescent boys to jump up and down for an hour. As if they could not jump up and down at home. This year he prefers such a thing to cakes, hats and songs; the domain of parties for little boys like Christopher Robin, little boys who are still more interested in stuffed animals than, for example, iPhones. I brought these boys to the trampoline gym, boys who don't mind the noise there—who don't know what silence is, who haven't been raised wandering the woods with a dull hatchet looking for logs to hack just because. Boys who spent the entire 90-minute drive talking about a video game in which you seek "gems" and "shards" and so forth, conversation my grandmother wouldn't begin to understand. If she were dead, she would roll over in her grave. But she is still alive. She has never sought a "shard" unless she broke a canning jar on the kitchen floor.

When I work around heavy machinery—beam saws, lawnmowers, CNC (computer numerical control) machines—I am religious about protecting my ears with these miraculous little pieces of key-lime green foam. That protects my physical ear, but the inner filters, the ones that say "unfamiliar is bad," those are harder to keep clear. Look at me: I already have begun to judge my son's pastimes as frivolous, and he's only 12. What will I think of his children's children? Will I be able to comprehend anything of what they do and how they choose to be?

In the fourth century, monks went into the wilderness to eschew sin (at least a few of the more common sorts of sin like pride and lust) and even to stay away from its on-ramps. Then they realized something new about the ascetic who marries, raises children, and transacts commerce. They realized this sort of believer has chosen the more difficult way to listen; the air is impure around him and he has less time to filter out the smog. It's harder for her to make space to hear God, it's harder for him to avoid the magnetic attraction of flesh. It's hard for her not to be talking when the bass solo begins. He is constantly interrupted, and prone to interrupting boorishness himself.

I want to be listening before the bass solo, before the quiet comes. We have to be listening while trampolines are full of children, and LeBron James is about to be on the NBA[43] *Sunday Showcase* on ESPN,[44] and the pizza parties, and clowns, and flashing lights all distract me from writing this down with any coherence.

And it might be justly criticized that I wrote an essay during my boy's birthday party instead of spending money (money we don't have) to go jump with him, but I think he's happy, chattering with his friends, bounding about like Tigger in *Winnie the Pooh.* But I know something's going on between his ears. Perhaps his thoughts are muddled today like poor old Pooh, but someday he'll begin to talk about what he thinks with clarity. Like, how I'm wrong. He already points out that my desk is messy, but the day will come when he questions everything I believe; not just my external habits, but how I choose to *be.* That will be his bass solo, his chance to see if I'm listening.

And I know I am happy, sitting here, writing about learning to listen, thinking about how much I love him and how I want to be dedicated to keeping my filters clean so that I can truly listen to even his grandchildren someday, if I can last that long in this prematurely rusty car that is my body. To be listening to him before the bass solo begins, so that when he finally starts talking to me about things he's discovering—what is God, or what is woman, or why didn't you make much money during this phase when I wanted you to love me by buying stuff—that I won't be laughing in the background of the recording like a clown and miss his moment. I don't want to be caught blaring away when the time comes to listen to my son whose voice has somehow dropped into the bass register by the time I edit this article six months later, a boy who looks so much like I do that my childhood friends' eyes pop when they see him. But he really isn't like me in many ways, he's much quieter, much more tidy, he prefers running lights and I prefer to be the guy on stage, he's more the bass and I'm more the trumpet. If jazz is going to be any good, the trumpet player *has to listen* to the bass and piano and drums.

One day it will be quiet enough for him that he will feel he's ready for the bass solo to begin, and I hope to be ready. The wax is out of my ears, or so it is as I have dreamed.

- ❖ What are you doing when the bass solo emerges from the noise that is your friends' life?

- ❖ What will it mean for you to be an aficionado?

- ❖ Who will you stop impressing so that you can start listening to the band?

Failure first

In 2009, my very first assignment coaching a missionary was with a leader 20 years my senior who had spent two grueling decades persecuted, imprisoned, and putting his life and his family in danger just because he wanted to tell people good news. He was pretty burned out. I think he was hoping for someone older and wiser. Basically a mentor. But this guy was such a senior leader, I'm not sure there was anyone left who could mentor him. There wasn't anyone who had been through anything worse. He was peerless.

The worst I had seen in terms of dangerous cross-cultural experience was a mild student demonstration in Zaire as a missionary's kid in 1988. I remember the way the students marched with placards and chanted; that day they were looking for one particular student, a youth who managed to hide from the mob and probably saved his own life by doing so. They found his bicycle, a most prized and valuable possession, and they torched it, beat it with wooden rods until it was beyond repair, and threw it over the net-less soccer goalposts on the official town pitch. Who knows how he offended them?

Also I remembered the psychological strain of knowing that a missionary had once been shot by rebels, martyred in 1964 when he landed his plane here in this town. Did I have cause to worry? Was this mob going to turn into a rebel army overnight? Would our family be in danger? And all through the riot that day, my mother wondered where my little sister was!

I didn't have much to go on with this senior leader I was supposed to coach, but as we told each other our life stories, I did my best to build rapport. I don't remember my exact words, but it must have been something like, "So I know what you're going through." But that little demonstration I casually observed as though I was watching a soccer match compared in no way to the imprisonment and abuse he'd suffered.

He almost screamed at me: "You have NO IDEA how DIFFICULT my life has been!" He was right. I was shocked at my blunder. I apologized and offered to get him reassigned to another coach. He declined a reassignment, but the rest of our six sessions were an uphill battle. I felt discouraged and insecure about my abilities, so I told my supervisor, "I don't know if I can do this." She laughed and said, "Oh, Adam, you're a well-trained coach, you're going to be just fine." What a relief to know that coaches have a value for believing in people. That has stuck with me because it was applied to me when I failed!

Whether you are learning to become a coach or just a better listener, you will fail. You will say something stupid when you open your mouth and use your tongue. It is a rather tricky rudder to wield, after all. Don't give up. Apologize, go back to listening.

❖ When did you first realize that you still had a lot to learn about listening?

Tom Sawyer and Huckleberry Finn

For we are what he has made us,
Created in Christ Jesus for good works,
Which God prepared beforehand to be our way of life.
—Ephesians 2:10, NRSV

M y friend Mark Garratt once observed, back when I was a young man, that I'm one of the biggest risk takers he knows. I'm no adrenaline junkie. There's no motorcycle in my garage. I don't go skydiving. What he's pointing to is my capacity for creative risk and making risky career moves. It's how I live as an artist and as an entrepreneur. I'm not afraid of hard work, particularly when it has great potential to pay off big. There's some truth to what he says.

A lot of risks that people take become, in retrospect, something they would have regretted NOT doing. For most of us, the pain of not trying first has to outweigh the fear of failure before we can even begin. We have to be able to visualize something pretty far down the road to take that step when we're comfortable, or we have to be willing to consider risk from the perspective of adventuresome play. This has very little to do with whether or not the thing works out in your favor. The first thing about risk is that it's polar opposite—the thing you get if you don't take the risk is regret. The stronger the urge to take a risk becomes, the greater the potential for regret if you don't try. Sometimes the most painful moment of leaping is when we've thought about it for too long imagining all the possible ways it could fail, dragging ourselves through the failure emotionally. If we fail, we only have to go through that again. But I believe we can condition ourselves through imaginative *play* to help ourselves more willingly come to the leaping point.

Because the truth is expanding, any play or fiction has the possibility of becoming real. Therefore, one approach to taking risks, living without fear, and going after a life that won't fill you with regret someday is the Tom Sawyer approach.

The two title characters in the books *Tom Sawyer* and *The Adventures of Huckleberry Finn* present a delightful contrast. Tom laughs in the face of danger. For Tom, there are few adventures that happen apart from his considerable imagination. It's interesting to note that the first truly treacherous event in Tom's life (when he and his sweetheart Becky get lost in a cave) doesn't fundamentally change his character; by the time we get back to him at the end of *Huck Finn,* he's back to his old shenanigans. In fact, simply because Tom likes to pretend to be something he's not (something far more glamorous), he ends up attempting a rescue operation at the end of the book much more the hard way than necessary.

In chapter 42, Tom and Huck discuss their attempt to free the runaway slave Jim.

Tom says, "We did set him free—me and Tom [Tom and Huck have switched identities, so when Tom refers to "Tom", he's referring to Huck]. We laid out to do it, and we done it. And we done it elegant, too."[45]

In terms of elegant, Tom is referring to the fact that he took a bullet in the leg. This is his idea of elegance. A pirouette on the pinhead of life on the grand scale of the matador. But on the next page, we find that Tom's flair for elegant put everyone unnecessarily in danger. Tom finds out that his "elegant" rescue attempt came to nothing, because the slave, Jim, has been caught again and is locked up.

> "They hain't no right to shut him up. Shove!—And don't you lose a minute, Turn him loose! He ain't no slave; he's as free as any cretur that walks this earth!"
>
> "What does the child mean?"
>
> "I mean every word I say, Aunt Sally ... Old Miss Watson died two months ago, and she was ashamed she ever was going to sell him down the river, and said so; and she set him free in her will!"[46]

Figure 12. Huckleberry Finn as depicted by E.W. Kremble in the original 1884 edition of the book.

So it turns out that Tom's entire rescue operation was a fantasy for him. The freedom was already given months before. The elegant escape was a game.

Once Huck figures this out, he's astonished. It is significant that Huck Finn, who has endured much more abuse at the hands of his father, typically sees the danger as real and the game as an illusion, as though he were prematurely an adult, while Tom doesn't. To Tom, the game is real, and the dangers are illusions. For Huck, the games are a waste of time from the useful procurement of food and shelter and other forms of safety. Because of the way he's been abused, Huck thinks and acts most of the time like an adult. He's the archetypical character who has seen more than a boy his age ought to have seen. Huck takes risks when he has no other choice. Tom takes real risks throughout the course of his fantasy.

But which is the better way to approach risk? Huck's approach is born out of reaction to abuse. He mitigates risk whenever possible in favor of self-preservation. The only thing that seems to overrule this approach is when he recognizes that others have been abused. In the most ironic and poignant passage in either novel, Huck decides to risk helping Jim escape, even though he knows, as he says, it's wrong. In this case, his internal moral compass overrules dictates from the social construct (which has never been much help to Huck anyway). So it's not that Huck won't take risks, he's just more careful for his own skin. The abuse taught him that life isn't a game. When we step out and take a risk seeing mostly danger, and disengage our imaginations for what could be, God says, "You keep using that word 'risk.' I do not think it means what you think it means. I have already set Jim, the slave, free." The Tom Sawyer approach where reality is the illusion and the game is real may look crazy, but it's the way to go.

The truth of our reality is so slight in comparison with the ever-expanding truth of possibility.

In the board game *Risk*, the attacker (the one taking a risk) gets three dice while the defender (usually the more conservative of the two players) gets only two dice but wins when there's a draw. A tie? Is that what you're hoping for? Why, it's simply un-American! The game's design plays on American impatience.

In the Western story, there is a beginning, middle, and end, and the theme almost always revolves around redemption. Redemption is never a tie. All things may be equal, but someone has to win. I suspect this is why we haven't been too quick to adapt to soccer. There are too many matches which end in a draw and we fail to appreciate the subtle tension in a draw.

For the adventurer, the bold risk taker, what could be more valuable than some instructive scenes from *The Princess Bride*?

The Man in Black outwits Vizzini in a famous scene where they engage a battle of wits to the death. One will drink from a poisoned cup and the other won't. It seems that the Man in Black is taking a 50/50 chance with his own life, but in reality he's immune.

There's no risk in this risky life. In many ways, we have that same immunity. Reality isn't what it seems—that is, reality limits the possible true outcomes and keeps us from embracing risk. Reality is more than meets the eye—not less. The risk is an illusion. The reality is much safer than it looks.

Later on in the film, the heroes execute what may be the riskiest rescue attempt ever.

When Fezzik growls, "The Dread Pirate Roberts is here for your souls!" as the Spaniard lights him on fire, the hundred men guarding the gate scatter, and yet, behind the scenes, there is not much holding him up. When we, the actors on our own stage, know that we have only just revived from being mostly dead like Westley; or shaken from a drunken stupor like Inigo; or we are semi-inarticulate, propped upon a wobbly wheelbarrow, like Fezzik; we can easily feel that our risk is built upon a sham. The reality we know about ourselves, however, is the illusion. When we take risks, we almost always feel like we're bluffing. The bigger reality is that our risk gives us the key to success.

What we see of ourselves when we are behind the scenes is no match for how God sees us—it is His vision to take the risk of propping us on a wheelbarrow, cloaking us and setting us on fire. He sees us as the one who can go and take souls for His sake and unlock the gate. In fact, we are playing a liberate-the-slave game like Tom Sawyer did, a game in which the real freedom was granted long ago. But we have to take the risk: stand up, light the cloak and speak the script with confidence. We have to be willing to be on fire. That part isn't a bluff at all.

When we recognize that the expanded truth, the thing which we can't see from our normal perspective, is not based on the visible reality, then our works are based on God's risk, not our own. God takes the risk on us! Then the good works which are supposed to be our way of life are the game that is real, and the dangers become illusions.

Finally, we notice that leaders who see reality as an illusion and the world in which we are already set free as reality are the types we want to follow.

It's so important for motivational listeners to lead by example in this way. We look to our leaders to say, "If even they can wobble on wheelbarrows to recover keys to the castle and they are willing to take a bullet in the leg, so can I!"

❖ How can you listen, live, work and play as though the slave were already freed?

Article 29

Ordinary superstars

Leadership means setting an example. When I was a high school cross country runner, Coach Mark could outrun and outwork all the boys on the team:

1. He led from the front; he could talk about speed and endurance with integrity. He knew how to get there, so you trusted he could help you get there too.
2. He could visualize our team running in the state competition and he talked about it often; he made sure that we knew what he thought we were capable of; and we did it. I ran at State both my junior and senior years.
3. Mark was tough. He could chew us out when our performance lacked, and he had the credibility to do this without causing mutinous reactions. That's partly because he only chewed us out about once per year, and mostly because we knew he had our best interest in mind.
4. Coach Mark was playful. His favorite stunt was to jog by a farmhouse with us, chatting casually about how sometimes a dog would come barking from that farmhouse's yard. Then, a few minutes later, he'd sneak up behind one of the runners, reach down and grab their calf with a bark. Some of the kids could have won a high-jump competition right then and there.

5. He took ordinary people with average athletic ability and turned them into competitors insofar as sheer effort could take an average athlete. (The proof of this I found out when I got to the college level! My effort could not hold a candle to the superior genetics a lot of those college athletes had.)

But there are usually only one or two true superstars on any team of elite athletes, or only one or two superstars on any regional sales team. The rest of the team, those of us with only average ability at our level, have to be led by someone we can fall into step behind. No matter what team you lead, you must take a superstar or two and blend them with a group of average performers who trust your guidance. This happens again at each level. Your average high school performers become the slower ones in college, and there's a new group in the "average" range. It happens again at the professional level.

As a high school athlete, I had average talent. I consider myself a writer of average ability (as James A. Michener once said, "I'm not a very good writer, but I'm an excellent rewriter"[47]) and I have to work hard to produce something valuable. It doesn't come easily the way shooting hoops seems to come to someone like Michael Jordan. Michael once told Al Franken's character Stuart Smalley on *Saturday Night Live*, who was attempting to motivate and affirm him by telling him it's OK if you aren't the best—"But Stuart, I *am* the best." At least, that's how I remembered it. Jordan never actually said that on the show, but he sure implied it with his thinly-disguised grin, or perhaps the laughter gave it away. But this is the biggest mistake we all make: God-given talent is one thing, but nobody achieves their maximum potential without effort, and Michael Jordan is the same way.

I don't think leadership is always about being the best. Michael Jordan led a team on the court very well but he ended up being widely criticized as a poor evaluator of talent.

It's difficult to evaluate talent when you are (or were at one time) the best. Your experience tells you that if people are hard workers, they rise to the top, but when you evaluate those with less talent, you're not sure how to judge what they might be able to achieve. Most people have to craft their team from average talent and even from average efforts (such as those we get from people who volunteer for our non-profit or church). People are sometimes giving their second- or third-best efforts to our team, for any number of reasons, all of which begin with the words *personal priorities.* A skill that includes all the other stuff Coach Mark used to do; taking those average people, finding out what motivates them, and molding them into a team. A superstar or two plus a team of average talent plus above-average effort and prioritization equals team performance.

Jesus didn't pick the most promising leaders from the best rabbinical schools. His vision was so different from the training model of the day that He had to pick complete outliers. The surprise was that within three years, He turned them into a winning team—and they never had a practice session that went very well. If you have a superstar on your team, that's great. But victory can be had without it.

P.S. He's done it again. October 31, 2015: Coach Mark, with my brother, Aaron, as his assistant coach, have taken the Mid-Prairie High School (Wellman, Iowa) boys *and* girls team to the State meet, placing fourth and eighth respectively in the meet. The reason it's worth mentioning is that the principles that guide their approach to coaching athletes give them consistently competitive teams year after year.

❖ Who's the average performer on your team?

❖ How can you elicit the best that they can give so that the team is a winning team?

Article 30

She burns my ears

Some time ago, I encountered an elderly Amish man in my office, I mean, in the local coffee shop. He was eager to talk to strangers which is rare for an Amish man, and I struck up a conversation. I sat and listened.

I learned that his many children were grown and some had left the state; people don't realize how much the Amish are on the move, taking rocky ground in Missouri, Wisconsin, Kentucky, and upstate New York and making something of it, starting new communities. When you don't own a petroleum-driven vehicle, even coming into "Goshen Town" is a long trip. But they do use Amtrak and hire vans so they can visit each other. I discovered that this man's first wife had died, and that he'd remarried against the advice of his community. His second wife was a long-time bachelorette, and he was her first husband. I'm sure they were both over 60 when they married. Therefore she was a good deal more independent than a normal Amish wife, and even though "they warned me," he said, "she burns my ears." Suddenly, I understood why he was talking to strangers.

My father-in-law sold agricultural products, fertilizers, etc., in Lancaster County, Pennsylvania (densest concentration of Amish in the world) all his life. He's 78 years old, lived around the Amish all his life, and he's never heard an Amish man talk like this. Never. He was never an insider as far as the Amish are concerned, but he wasn't enough of an outsider for them to open up that way. After all, he knew them and knew their neighbors. He might have kept a secret if asked, but he wasn't to be trusted. He was "English." As of we English have some odd spin on us, like a pool cue.

What allowed this exchange to happen? I wasn't too busy to listen. That's the first piece. You have to slow down if you want these sort of encounters. The second remarkable thing here is that the man lived in a "we-told-you-so" community where there was not a single empathetic ear for his problems with his second wife, so he took it outside the community. I was far enough outside his community that word couldn't travel back. I asked his name at one point and he wouldn't give it.

If you want to develop authentic community, you have to refrain from creating a "we-told-you-so" culture. When people take their problems away somewhere, going "off to town" to find an outlet, it makes restoration and reconciliation difficult. For an Amish man to share his story with me seems rather harmless, but there's potential for a much darker side to this phenomenon.

Also, if you want to hear what an Amish guy has to say, you have to be lucky and keep your mouth shut.

❖ The next time you're tempted to say, "I told you so," stop. Don't do it. Do this five more times, ten times. Hold that judgment back. Note how it impacts your relationships.

۞

To lower your risk of hearing damage,
do not listen at high volume for long periods.
—My Smart Phone

۞

Take this advice seriously, both physically with your music/media and in your relationships with people who are prone to shouting at you!

Protect your hearing when using noisy industrial machinery. I spent many years in an industrial shop with high-pitched saws, cutting wood products. I wore ear plugs EVERY single day. I wear them still when mowing my lawn. Lose your hearing, and listening will become much more difficult!

۞

Article 31

The Pileated Woodpecker

Whatever catches my client's attention is a jumping-off point for a line of questions, an analogy to their situation.

Today my client turned and looked out the window. "There's a Pileated Woodpecker outside," he said. "I haven't seen one for many years."[48]

I don't want to over-spiritualize the idea of getting "a sign" but it's a place to be creative and play. We began to relate the Pileated Woodpecker to his situation.

Where's the Pileated Woodpecker in your context?

Figure 13. The Pileated Woodpecker.

He recognized an item he hadn't been working on for a long time but had been an aspect of his organization's past that he was thinking needed to be brought to the forefront again.

What makes a Pileated different from other woodpeckers, the normal ones? They're bigger. More rare. Something seen before but very distinctive.

What is the distinctive thing your organization needs right now? He identified a certain type of person who could help his organization.

The client developed some things he thought related. In fact, his energy level increased as we spoke. Finally, I said, "What does you using your binoculars look like in terms of keeping a lookout for someone like this who could help you?"

He spoke for a while and eventually said, "I need to share about the Pileated Woodpecker with my team."

"So, the team is your binoculars? They help you see a depth of field that you couldn't see otherwise?"

"YES!"

I like to play off my client's surroundings, especially things they take special note of. Use them as creative places to ask weird, off-the-wall questions. See what happens and trust the process. It's OK for my client to go looking out the window, as long as I'm standing ready to ask them to apply what they see in a principle.

❖ Next time you're tempted to try to get somebody back on track, try following their roundabout path instead. Ask them how what they've noticed might relate.

Article 32

Sundaes on Saturday

What does it mean to live in the present, to hear each other in the present, to be known in the present, to be present with one another? The past seems so concrete, and the future so ethereal, but the moment itself, how do you even begin to live there?

A few weeks after I returned from a trip to Asia, my family gathered on a Saturday night, and my in-laws were in town from out of state. Grandpa John bought a lot of ice cream with all the toppings you can imagine, and the kids were enjoying sundaes.

I turned to my son Benjamin, a few days shy of seven years old at the time, and asked him, "How is it that we're having sundaes but it's only Saturday? Can you explain this?"

Without missing a beat, he said, "It's already Sunday, in Thailand." And he was right. It was about 7:00 AM tomorrow in Bangkok.

When I think about the paradoxical idea that the kingdom is coming and the kingdom is now, I realize that this time-zone phenomenon is part of our everyday reality, and it's a perfect example of living in the present while the future is already here. Living in that present is as easy as eating a sundae on a Saturday night.

❖ What are you concerned about for tomorrow that's already taken care of today?

Article 33

In just a moment

The act of listening to another human says something words cannot say. "You are valued. What's in your heart is worth hearing, and what's in the deepest part of your spirit—your biggest dreams—are important. Your past is meaningful. And your *now* is worth sharing." When we talk about listening in this way, we talk about "being present." In this sort of listening, there is less concern for asking questions. I'm interested in the question of what the present *is*.

A long pause in a conversation—after the last thing was said, yet before the next words are spoken—this is (one definition of) the present.

Common tips to being present are not reading text messages while with others, finding a private place to talk uninterrupted, and so on. These good suggestions are preparation for being focused in the present moment, but they are not the act of being in the moment. So what really is the present? Isn't it even more difficult to define than the past or the future?

In the Genesis void, there was no past—certainly, not as we know and define it and feel it in our memories now. As for the future during that Genesis void, future was going to be a thing only if God would so decide. This might happen any time, but didn't, for so long as God decided, "Void." God is, eventually and after all is said and done, a God of Yes. This God only had to decide "Yes" once for there to be something else: a future extending away from the past, a universe expanding through time as well as space.

We hold those we are truly listening to in a place where we recreate the void—unconcerned about what we did before we got here, or what comes next. This present moment is a place to store hope, like a trap door into a secret room where we can put a dream down on the table and leave it untouched, unhandled, until we're ready to come back. In this secret void room, this space we create for people, they can put down their visions and know we won't trifle with them. They can come back to them later, in another moment, and find them there.

When God said yes, the void that happens in the present began to be a thing separate from past or future:

"Let there be light."[49]

Light travels at 186,282 miles per second which makes our own reaction times look pathetic. I suggest that we might as well not use the present to try to react. To recreate the void for people is not to react anyway.

Is "the present" that moment between when the color of light hits our eye and the moment we react? Or broader? Is it today—this time I've been writing (and surfing the net) since I sat down at the coffee shop about 90 minutes ago? As long as I hang on to this moment between walking in the door and walking back out? Is it the time between when one friend comes to greet me at this table, breaking my concentration for a few minutes, and when the next one does an hour later? How long, spiritually, is a moment?

The action of light moving and the reaction of the heart beating in response makes a present moment; some Eastern philosophers talk of it as a breath—inhaling and exhaling, a cyclical experience of now.

I'm not quick—my reaction time today averages only 369 milliseconds. The fastest human recorded reacts at 101 milliseconds. Chances are you are quicker than I am—I am only in the fifteenth percentile on www.humanbenchmark.com. Does this just mean my present moment lasts longer than most peoples' moments do?

In baseball, the coaches strategize and think ahead—not only concerned with how their players may be deployed best for today, but for the rest of the week; the coach is concerned with performance over time. The coach must concern himself constantly with how what happens today impacts tomorrow's game. He's constantly speculating.

The best radio announcers tell anecdotes of the past days when baseball was in infancy, or in her golden years, when her fields were filled with daisies and her players ran home in the dusk when the light failed. A time before steroids and gambling, before electricity and before the $18 hot dog. Announcers work in the present moment, but there is plenty of space in their dialogue for reminiscing.

In the meantime, players play best when they play in the present. The present—that moment between the time when the ball leaves the pitcher's hand and the moment when it hits something (the catcher's mitt, the dirt, the backstop, the batter's knee, the umpire's mask) or is struck by the bat (shifting the ball's trajectory into passive voice). For the players, baseball hasn't changed and isn't going to change. Only their reaction time and raw speed will change. Their time for peak performance is now; the time to swing or not to swing is now. Now is the time for outfielders to crash into the fence to catch a ball, unconcerned about whether or not they will be able to play tomorrow. Their only focus is catching the ball in this moment. Base runners collide with the catcher at home; a moment is all they have, it's the only thing in their hands.

Everything is happening in the stillness of that moment—that curveball spinning on an arc in space is a metaphor for a world waiting for its own destiny. And the entire park is attentive to it—or at least those viewers who are initiates into the beauty of a breathless moment, waiting like all creation, straining "on tiptoe to see the wonderful sight of the sons of God coming into their own."[50]

That's a great vision for us as listeners: we are the audience holding our collective breath to see what might happen now.

"Now," Jesus says, "I will sit here with you while the earth spins and the heavens wait with bated breath to see what is in your future drawer."

People don't often realize what a tool listening is for sharing Jesus with the world. We too can say:

"I will sit here with you, standing in for Jesus, while the earth spins and the heavens wait to see you come into your own."

To hold the moment and keep holy the space in which we listen, we must react without flinching and keep still! We must react not too early, nor too late, and sometimes, not at all.

❖ In which situation or relationship right now can you consciously choose not to react and just wait to see how someone will come into their own?

A green duck

My daughter discovered guessing games. After I guessed her riddle of "What *am-immal* lives in a jungle?" it was my turn to think of an animal, her turn to guess.

I said, "I'm thinking of an animal that lives in a pond. Can you guess?"

"I KNOW! A DUCK!"

"No, it's not a duck. I'll give you a hint. It's green."

"OH! IT'S A *GREEN* DUCK!"

In her defense, my daughter sees a lot of a *blue* pond-dwelling character named Duck on a PBS animated series (the show is called Peep). She knows other *am-immals* but her mind is especially fixated on "Duck." For a minute, she really couldn't see anything else. (Until I said, "Ribbit.")

Too often our worldview is so limited that when presented with other options to explore, we use those options to redefine and narrow down our initial ideas even more, rather than expanding our vision for what truths we may not have seen before. Green ducks exist, so while my daughter's second guess still fits the perimeters of reality, she got no closer to the truth, because I confirmed it wasn't a duck! This is the

Figure 14. "A Green Duck" by Mark Daniels.

sort of thinking that creates barriers between ourselves and others. A pond is a diverse place. Many species of frogs, snakes, dragonflies, and turtles are green, and other options open up if we stop assuming the question pertains only to a pond in Midwestern North America. What about an Amazonian pond, or a frozen pond on Mars? Polarized thinking begins when we stop at our first assumption of the meaning of a thing, and the thinking becomes more and more fundamentalist as we link additional facts to support our initial conclusion, theory, or meaning. When new information gets presented ("It's not a duck.") we reject it, and instead of opening up to unlimited possibilities again, we cling to our first take on the topic. Our certainties then become even more highly detailed ("It's a *green* duck."). The certainties, which would have plausibly been correct before the new information came along are now woefully lacking to the point of making us look like fools as we short-circuit the expansion of our imagination in favor of what we "know." In other words, even when given new information, we take a Black Swan, perhaps, and paint it white. Or maybe it isn't as impacting as a Black Swan event. Maybe it's just any "ol' pond am-mimal," and we paint it green and call it a duck.

We encounter those who dam their pond and take a vat of green paint to their ducks, and with it all of pond life has been transformed from a multifaceted mystery into a monochromatic, poisonous factoid: our book says this, and we can allow no new discovery to inform our views. There is a certain justification writers get when they see their work in print—on paper. When we respond and quote their work to disprove it, we're giving voice to something perhaps best ignored. There is a point when we stop listening, and a point when we stop quoting and arguing: it is the point when the speaker begins painting ducks green.

Yes, it's true that there ARE green ducks (around here, they're usually married to brown ones). There are also many other things which live in ponds; some green, some not. There are ducks which aren't green. Adding details to your thesis doesn't make it more plausible or even more correct, and while it might contain a correct fact, it could be missing the broader truth. Narrow-minded approaches like this polarize people un-necessarily, alienate people and misses the broadest possibility of the beauty of truth: the fact that what we do know is far out-weighed by what we don't.

❖ Where is what you do know outweighed by what you don't?

❖ What assumptions are you making?

❖ Who can reveal your blind spots?

Listening is not magical

A scholarly and scientific Christian religion based on the Bible without intersection with art, can tend toward the dogmatic because implicit in many expressions of art is the element of the mysteriousness of relationship with the divine. There are Bible scholars who can explain when and where (historical context) and social scientists/ ecclesiologists who explain how and what (application for today), but we need artists who can dance around the circumference of who and why without trying to explain Jesus and the rest of His very other type of family—God/Him/It/Her, or their holy collective purposes (the part we'll never be able to fully explain). So we need context, application and mystery: a reminder that these first two are only a shadow flickering on the wall, an observational sketch based on light from the fire inside the ring of dancers. (Scholars and scientists can be artists and dance too; there aren't hard lines separating the three.)

Art which doesn't embrace and dance with this other family and their purposes is susceptible to becoming propaganda, in other words, to celebrate a dogma or something else that is second-rate. Art must have freedom to acknowledge the mystery of the other family and purpose, even the abandonment to worship them. Rather than explain, art listens to the music, watches the fire, and searches for the dance steps, plays like children with sparklers, revels in awe and celebration, not considering or concerned that a final conclusion might or ought to be established. Children with sparklers and marshmallows embrace the mystery of fire and sugar and know only that their moment is bright and sweet.

So far I have discussed the dangers of faith and art operating on their own as being dogma and propaganda, respectively; both are manipulative in nature. Since my primary interest in the intersection of art and faith is in the area of the art of motivational listening, we are aware now that this art must be practiced with the dance steps that are danced in the circle of God and God's purpose. Listening to others without incorporating God is espionage (observation with intent to inform upon and control) or voyeurism (observation with intent to take our pleasure from the moment but not to give) and this ultimately will not prove motivating.

Instead, the art of motivational listening brings the intent to discover with awe the life before us, humans as enchanting as a spark and as fragile as a marshmallow. Listening can motivate towards God and God's purpose so that each person's spark and sweetness hits the mark of its purpose and isn't wasted. Involving Jesus in the conversation is a remarkable boon. Of course, everything Jesus does is remarkable. Jesus can set us on fire without consuming us—a marshmallow always flaming, never blackened. Listening for the motivation to come, to say, "Here am I, send me," and then the courage to go, is a deep privilege.

When we begin to learn to listen, we learn to give up control and our prayers take a different shape. Prayer without listening is an attempt at magic, to manipulate the spiritual elements and realm, to our own benefit.

To religiously practice art or to artfully practice religion without listening and prayer is either not possible or manipulative: dogmatic, propagandist, voyeurism, espionage and darkly magical. To practice the art of motivational listening without faith is only a subset. Motivation is found most easily when the listener is devoid of dogma, propaganda, espionage, voyeurism or/and sense of magic, or even briefly, any attempt to control the speaker's life.

❖ How are you giving up control today?

Article 36

General Awareness

Generaleneral Awareness was hiking through the woods when Major Distraction came zipping along in a jeep and caught up with him.

"What are you looking for, General?"

"Everything," replied the general, "and nothing in particular, just keeping my eyes open. At least, nothing I can really define right now. I'm sort of.... Wow, you got that jeep tricked out pretty sweet."

"Thanks for noticing! Yes, and it's faster than walking. You can get where you're going easily with it and find just about anything around here; want a ride? I can take you anywhere you want to go, and we can find whatever you're looking for! Look, up ahead, there's a great view of the valley," said the major bouncing in his seat.

"It's very nice, but, I think I'm looking for someone who's afoot; I think I'll have to walk just to remember what or who it is, and besides I think you have to sneak up on it," said the general.

The major roared away laughing. When he was gone, the general sat for a few moments gathering his thoughts. Then he gazed up into the trees. He looked at them one at a time, but soon, he saw the forest. "Ah, there you are," he said, "I knew you were right around here somewhere."

"Yes, I've been here all along, hiding in plain sight. But you can always find me just by being yourself," said a voice.

"You're always so good with your camouflage, Colonel O'Truth!" said the general with a smile.

"Would it be any fun to find me if I wasn't?" replied the colonel.

Article 37

Croquet

A s legend has it, in 1982 a midshipman bragged to Kevin Heyburn, then a St. John's freshman, that Navy could beat St. John's in any sport. Heyburn replied, "All right. Let's play croquet."

At our house, croquet looks a lot more like Calvinball, a game invented by the lead character in the comic strip *Calvin and Hobbes*, where the rules are always in flux and fun is the critical element. But the

Figure 15. Victorian croquet at the Mid-Atlantic Center for the Arts and Humanities, Cape May, NJ.

annual contest between Navy and St. John's is a serious affair, a cutthroat chess match with serious, tactical approaches and a court built on exacting parameters and governed by rules from aristocratic antiquity. The Johnnies have now defeated Navy 26 times in 33 years, winning the annual Annapolis Cup by a score of 3–2 in 2015. The players actually practice.

It takes guts to pick a niche the way Heyburn did. You have to be ready to admit your quirks and you may endure ridicule. But it's also possible that you'll make some great friends and have a lot of fun in the process.

Listeners are looking for relevance, which is harder than it usually appears. This is because most of our initial thoughts about why something is relevant to us is handed to us via a social construct which issues expectations, such as, "Let's compete in one of the four or five major sports." Instead of the more typical canned responses, we're looking for the croquet match challenge, that unique answer that comes not from any number of expected ideas but rather from a perspective that breaks down social norms in favor of owning the answer for oneself and therefore tackling a challenge on our own terms.

I know what I'm talking about: my hobbies are Vintage Base Ball (1860's rules: no gloves, no sliding, no spitting or cussing) and Scrabble®. Things I chose because I liked them and didn't care if others thought I was nuts—I like the people in the culture and I appreciate the etiquette as much as the competition, so that I find the hobbies relaxing.

Even the act of writing a book can present challenges. You're up against a world full of books. As Taleb points out, we've got a world where more and more is being said, and less and less of it is worth anything.[51] This book itself is my own attempt to add something to the literature of listening and coaching by inviting you to play croquet with me. I didn't want to write the book you may have expected to get. This is not a bait and switch. It's better than that. I hope that those who pick up the book expecting one thing will find that what they needed was really something completely different. The book itself is a surprising reply to your challenge to me. "Write me a book," you say, and I say, "OK, here's my un-canned response," and you either say, "Well, croquet it is, then," or, I suppose, you decide that you didn't want to take this challenge on after all.

"But when a writer plans something new, and conceives a different kind of reader, he wants to be, not a market analyst, cataloguing expressed demands, but, rather, a philosopher ... He wants to reveal to his public what it *should* want, even if it does not know it. He wants to reveal the reader to himself."[52]

And that, my friends, is the sum of authenticity and leadership. It is the invitation to play croquet.

The WHY behind writing non-fiction books is "because I'm building a platform" more often than "because I have something unique to say." As I write these paragraphs, I'm sitting at a table in my local bookstore. The best table happens to be in the religious section, so I can see names peering at me from the shelves such as Bill Hybels, Max Lucado, C.S. Lewis, Brian McLaren, Donald Miller, and Henri Nouwen, and that's just between H and N. It's easy to think we don't have anything to add, mainly because the more we try to add something that's *like* what's already there, the less valuable it is. We have to be willing to take a risk, to add a challenge to croquet to the mix, to play to our own quirky strengths. It doesn't matter if we're writing books, managing a charity, or offering landscape design, if we're like everybody else, we're beaten. If we think we have to match what's been done (say, to compete with Navy in football or basketball, or, worse yet, to compete against the midshipmen in naval warfare), we're already beaten. That's why they call it the "beaten" path—once you take that path others have pioneered, you're already beaten. Getting off the beaten path is our chance to win against immense odds (who am I up against—Hybels, Lewis and Nouwen?), and if Kevin Heyburn of St. John's University is any model, we should win at least 26 times out of 33.

So the motivational listener is looking for opportunities to encourage that crazy idea, that willingness to explore, to come up with a different approach. The first challenge is to not settle for pat answers. Usually the first reason we're given for why someone wants to do a thing isn't the core reason. We also have to help other people find their own croquet challenge with which they can dare the world and take on all comers.

❖ Where can you get a win by playing your own game?

The unwritten books

L ike Kurt Vonnegut's character Kilgore Trout (who doesn't write most of the books he conceives of), the books I write sometimes don't happen. I write a ton of material which gets relegated to the sidebar of my creativity, and they're only worth a paragraph or two in a real book. For example, I had an idea for a book titled *Jesus in Jeopardy*. The core idea was that we jeopardize peoples' ability to hear anything when we present Jesus as "The Answer" on bumper stickers. Instead of sloganizing Jesus, I suggested that we think of Jesus more like the answer on *Jeopardy!* (the popular television game show). *Jesus in Jeopardy* is Jesus as The Question.

What this had to do with listening was that we ought to ask people, "Who is Jesus to you?" And then shut up and listen. This book was about how religious people love to hand out easy answers instead of listening. Perhaps if anything I read inspired this, it was *Blue Like Jazz* in which Donald Miller talked about how a small group of Christians on the campus of a hedonistic college in Portland, Oregon set up a confession booth and proceeded to confess the sins that they, as part of the established Christian church, had committed against the broader culture to the party-prone students.[53]

I had another idea for a book called *Sourdough Motivation.*

I got inspired, initially, by Michael Pollan who was on the radio[54] talking about his book, *Cooked: A Natural History of Transformation.*[55]

He mentioned how sourdough bread is made. It was so interesting, I bought his book. In my book, I was going to talk about how if we want to have a culture in our business or nonprofit organization or church that is healthy and delicious, we ought to look at sourdough. I identified four things I thought we should cultivate if we want a sourdough culture which motivates our workers or volunteers: 1) an Epic Mythos, 2) Heterogeneity, 3) Authenticity, 4) A Meta-Strange Attractor (huh?).

Figure 16. *[Sourdough] Culture eats strategy for breakfast.*
—Peter Drucker [author's paraphrase]

First, the idea for Epic Mythos was that we ought to have a story and invite people to that purpose. In other words, we make the conditions ripe for people to want to join our journey and help create our story. Bakers sets up the right conditions for sourdough on their kitchen counters and they don't even have to populate the dough with micro-biotics. Bacteria materialize (scientists don't know where they come from) to inhabit the water and flour and begin to ferment a revolution to make dough for the baker. In other words, if you set up the right conditions in your business, you have an epic story just waiting for people to get on board, and they will.

Then I rambled on about Jason and the Argonauts (the original Greek myth where Jason leads a bunch of guys to Colchis, which is about where Sochi, Russia is today) and I blabbed about the Winter Olympics until I finally got down to, *What is your Golden Fleece, your Gold Medal?* We're inspired by a quest. That's what attracts people, just like the right environment attracts bacteria and yeasts out of thin air to a sourdough batch.

Second, while most bread made in the United States uses only one strain of yeast and a bunch of preservatives, sourdough is a self-perpetuating, heterogeneous culture where any harmful bacteria is put in its place by the good bacteria. Diversity is good. I decided that a culture where the minority opinion is valued and listened to very carefully had some crossover with the need for outside perspective.

I think of it the way people observe nation-states from without and within. As outsiders, the USA could see the problems South Africa had with Apartheid. As insiders, the African-American population and other minorities have a clear view of white privilege and other aspects of institutionalized racism even today in the USA, while many whites can't see it at all. The foreign observer sees certain things clearly. The internal minority does too, but they are also insiders to an extent.

Mark Whitacre was the FBI informant in the largest price-fixing scandal in the USA, ever. Mark wore a wire for the FBI gathering insider information for three years to set himself up for a plea bargain. He mentioned that in every meeting he was involved in, there was also a green lamp in the room. Paris, Hong Kong; same lamp in every meeting (hiding a camera) and none of the people who attended all these meetings noticed. They were all men. His joke is that if there'd been one woman in the group, she would have noticed that lamp and the gig would be up. My unproven theory that went the next step, was that with just one woman in the group adding a little bit more heterogeneity, it's possible that the group wouldn't have been doing illegal stuff in the first place (we can't be sure). Not because women have more integrity necessarily, but because I believe that heterogeneity, the voice of the minority, forces us to think twice about what we think is right; it *begs* integrity.

Third, for some reason I thought that sourdough bread, maybe because it's more *artisanal,* is authentic stuff, each batch unique, with its own strain, and preservatives aren't needed—all that hippie stuff. I had one decent thing to say about defining authenticity and one idea about how to implement authenticity:

> Authenticity is one of those things that is easier to identify when it is lacking. But it's very hard to define. In this respect, it is, I think a subset of Quality.

⁊◦◅

> "A few days later he worked up a definition of his own and put it on the blackboard to be copied for posterity. The definition was: 'Quality is a characteristic of thought and statement that is recognized by a non-thinking process. Because definitions are a product of rigid, formal thinking, quality cannot be defined.'
>
> "The fact that this 'definition' was actually a refusal to define did not draw comment. The students had no formal training that would have told them that his statement was, in a formal sense, completely irrational. ... When I say, 'Quality cannot be defined,' I'm really saying formally, 'I'm stupid about Quality.'"[56]

OK. So I'm stupid about Authenticity. But you need it if you want a Sourdough Cultural Revolution. I suggested one way most businesses and organizations could improve would be to have more authentic conversations about money, because as Dan Pink pointed out in *Drive*, money is the primary motivator for almost nobody, and most organizations do a terrible job at talking about money.[57] Then there were a bunch of bad puns about dough.

Last, the idea I called a "Meta-Strange Attractor" is a next level take I had on the ideas in a book called *Surfing the Edge of Chaos*. That idea was simply that once we conquer survival, we push ourselves back to the edge of chaos. To that idea, I added mine, that when we push ourselves back to the edge after conquering survival, we end up with existential angst, and when we conquer our angst, it is because we have realized that our purpose is to help someone else survive, the "meta-" portion:

Hungry for purpose, we are at odds with our environment precisely because the environment requires us first to survive, and we have overcome that challenge. Growth (and the survival that comes with it) in the conceptual age means that once we are comfortable, we must once again find a way to get uncomfortable. Yet when nothing else keeps us from the comfort of equilibrium, our quest for purpose and meaning takes over and again drives us to the edge of chaos. In his book, *Facing the Congo*, journalist Jeffrey Tayler described a dangerous 1,100 mile journey down the Congo River during the late 1990s, a shadowing of Henry Stanley's voyage about 100 years earlier, upon which he (Tayler) embarked for no great reason other than to seek meaning in life (then write a book about it). Tayler's quest became— spoiler alert—a journey which he ultimately abandoned early, short of his goal, for no reason other than the fact that he realized he was jeopardizing the life of his guide, whose sole motive for the journey was survival![58]

The Meta-Strange Attractor, where you push past equilibrium to find purpose feeds back into your Epic Myth, and there you go with your self-perpetuating culture. There were a bunch more ideas about flywheels and navigation and so forth. I gave one keynote speech on it for a Chamber of Commerce dinner in a nearby town, and I left my audience scratching their heads because I was an idiot and used about 880 points instead of a nice round number like 3. I think if someone wanted a Sourdough Motivation culture, they could work on those four things and they'd probably be in good shape. This book that I didn't write had more to do with motivation than listening. The idea is to begin creating a culture where people, like bacteria, could bring their own motivation to your organization to begin a Sourdough Cultural Revolution.

I had ideas about things like how flywheels and a steel railroad track work together to create inertia and decrease friction so you can pull more with less effort; but no ideas about how to get there.

I ended with how we navigate using the North Star which provides outside perspective. I started researching a Pacific islander named Tupaia who helped Captain Cook navigate without using any instruments, like some sort of mystical guru of navigation, because he didn't even have the North Star to guide him, but he knew the ocean so well he could sail hundreds of miles and end up at a particular island. Nobody could figure out how he could do it without landmarks. Then I was at a loss to explain how that might factor into our need for outside perspective except to say that sometimes you just need a native of the environment to guide you or you can get lost. That was my pitch for hiring coaches and finding mentors.

You just read two books by Kilgore Trout.

❖ What would it look like in your life to present questions more than offer answers?

❖ How can you implement sourdough motivation?

❖ Of the four core ideas, which do you need to implement most in your organization?

Article 39

Time travel

*Being motivated to make a change is more important
than knowing what change to make.
Change is more a function of motivation than information.*[59]
—Tony Stoltzfus

Strategic sessions will have been in vain if your culture is toxic. Strategy gets eaten alive by the toxicity of a cannibalistic culture.

A positive (or "sourdough") culture (see Article 38), on the other hand, will eat strategy for breakfast, too, as a nourishing thing and use that strategy to fuel its self-perpetuating growth. It will have a delicious breakfast for itself, and in turn make pancakes for you, too!

More and more of us are juggling slash careers, working multiple jobs. It's becoming difficult to keep people working for you engaged for the long term. Business leaders are always looking for better ways to keep their best employees—and themselves—motivated. Your best employees aren't just motivated by money. There's a huge entrepreneurial spirit in our nation, and it is only getting stronger. Many people mistakenly believe that if they could simply access the right information, it would change their life for the better. But accessing the right information isn't enough. You also have to access it *at the right time.* It's worthless if you knew it and forgot, or knew it and didn't apply it for any reason, or if you only find out the information you needed after the fact. In the age of Google, we still end up thinking, "I should have said...."

That's because accessing the right information at the right time isn't always possible, even with the Internet on your smart phone. In the leadership coaching world, it is said that motivation is a function of relationship, not of information. But we still buy and sell books because we still place some trust in the idea that information which comes in a book is a particular kind of accessible (inexpensive) way to resource our learning and growth.

Implementation of this idea that the right information would change your life for the better as long as you can access and properly apply it at the right time requires time travel. The closest thing I know to real time travel is to send ideas forward in time by writing. As I write, my future reader is in mind; as you read you find that I am writing from your past. Welcome to my time machine!

Our desire to implement the right information at the right time is a testament to the popularity of time-travel movies.

"Though most would cite H.G. Wells's 1895 novel *The Time Machine* as the progenitor of the modern time-travel story, the author wrote an even earlier one, 'The Chronic Argonauts,' in 1888. Sandwiched between Wells's two time-machine stories was the other founding text of the genre: Mark Twain's 1889 satire *A Connecticut Yankee in King Arthur's Court....* The fact that it took so long for a non-adapted time-travel story to become a mainstream hit is a testament to how difficult films like these are to write. Every time-travel tale needs to establish its own internally consistent set of rules, and hardcore genre fans—a notoriously pedantic bunch—will tear apart any story that fails to do so... [In] the early 1980s... filmmakers like James Cameron (*The Terminator*) and Robert Zemeckis (*Back to the Future*) discovered an ingenious solution to the near-impossibility of writing a sensical [sic] time-travel story: Write a time travel story that's so much fun mainstream audiences won't care about consistency... They succeeded, in part, because they found the balance between science—enough, in fact, to keep diehard genre fans working out its logic for decades—and story."[60]

These movies are often based on the premise that, "If I knew yesterday what I know now, my situation would be better." Then we ask this: "Or would it be better, really?" That's the deeper question which the better of these time-travel flicks pose. A satisfying time travel movie always leaves you scratching your head, because there is ultimately no way to resolve the final chord in the symphony of the plot to a harmonious one—the logic always falls through somewhere. And so in the time-travel genre, accessing the right information at the right time is shown to be not only impossible even with a time machine (once an action is retroactively corrected there's always another layer of how it might have played out *even better!*) but usually it's also portrayed as dissonant, unsatisfying and undesirable. We must not miss the point at the end of the quote above: the power of story to draw fans from outside the diehard genre crowd. We don't care if it isn't realistic so long as it's a good story.

The reality is that our relationship to the right information suffers because the constraint time puts upon us comes with a certain necessity to act and react only in the moment. Only now do we act, only now do we react. Never in the past or future. So often that action or reaction is sadly uninformed. So be it. Even time travel isn't working. Even books. We write them in hope, we read them in hope, but even the books with the most correct information possible are not as effective as a relationship. How, then, do we change and grow? How do we stay motivated in spite of the ceaseless ticking of the clock dragging us kicking and screaming into every new and uninformed moment? Hang the future! The future is the time when all our super-strategies collapse under the Kryptonite of something unforeseen, something life changing, as small as a scratch on your leg which becomes infected, or as large as the birth of a child or death of a close relative. I hold this truth to be self-evident: that all of us are created equal and must deal with things in the moment as best we can.

Does this mean I'll never again coach someone through the process of creating a SMART (Specific, Measurable, Attainable, Relevant and Time-Oriented) goal? Of course not. Strategizing for the future will always be important. But one thing always trumps strategy. That thing is *culture*: and a culture may be defined as the story of purposeful relationships. A true understanding of culture compiles values and past experience and tells a story about that culture's own expected future, which in turn impacts the present action. It is a story that motivates us. The relationships which are most important, the things which are relevant to our cultural values, these things move us when we must act or react, when we don't have time to stop and decide whether or not we're even working with the right information.

Is this part of the paradox: that the desired future could inform action in the present as much as the past events do, or even more? Does living in the moment mean that we approach each step more as a step of faith for what the future can hold than as a reaction to what the past has given us? Are we being pushed ahead into the future by the past shoving up behind us, or does the future draw us gracefully into itself like a partner pulling us off the wall and onto the dance floor?

As for me, I presented this book not because I thought any of my ideas or philosophy would provide any information that's not already in the literature of the coaching movement. I hoped that some people who are truly motivated to become better listeners might use it to reflect upon that which drives them.

❖ What dreams do you have for your relationships in the future?

❖ How will you "write a story" of purposeful relationships to form the culture you envision?

❖ Review your values. What's relevant to you to work towards?

❖ What most motivates you to get there?

Article 40

Effective leaders

Leading your culture by living artfully makes you a better listener. Here are four things I believe will position leaders to do this in the twenty-first century. They are very tiny seeds of an idea now. Who knows? Perhaps I will develop them into a book. If not, this will be another of those Kilgore Trout moments.

1. Refined Complexity
Seeking cultural variety and keeping it in balance prepares you to specialize but maintain the healthy aspects of what it means to be a generalist. Draw from a variety of sources and use that to inform your culture. Then, as you strategize within a specialty, you're less likely to miss something important that's happening outside your usual focus.

2. Facing Pain
Savoring bitterness born of dry experiences builds character. Usually we don't think of savoring bitterness, but savoring in this sense is knowing something intimately and reflecting on how it impacts you. I promised not to talk much about character in this book, but examining bitter experiences rather than trying to ignore or bury them is one way to live artfully.

3. Engaging Risk

Narrow escape from the precipice of regret means that you've made a willing sacrifice somewhere along the line. That willing sacrifice of your comfort when it's easier not to take a risk will help you step back from the danger of that cliff. There is an illusion that staying near to comfort will leave us a life without pain, but we're balanced and ready to face pain. So our next move is to take a risk. One day we can look back on that risk and realize that the more dangerous path led to regret. We will be glad we went toward the risk instead, and so will those we lead there.

4. Seek Truth

The unexpected element of real freedom. Real freedom is not about what you can or cannot do, by law, or by religious restraint. Real freedom is about becoming who you can become within the expanding scope of truth rather than in spite of it. Experiencing this real freedom as we become something that reflects our full potential will bring us back around to a more refined complexity, lead to facing further pain (because the quest for truth will again become bitter before it becomes sweet) and then delicious again on the other side of new risks faced and regrets avoided.

My biggest fear is regret, and my biggest regret is living in fear. Those things are neither refined nor complex—they are raw. They are painful in a way that shames us so that we look away rather than facing it. They suck us into themselves and we forget to take the next risk, to seek truth the next time around, because we are in the cyclical grip of regret and fear.

❖ Begin at the beginning: variety, balance, complexity, and refinement.

Slowly moving rivers

I walked by the mill-race today, and the water moved lazily past me. It was almost as if the river said to me, "I have nowhere to go in particular, but something magnetic compels me into motion."

I, too, was stuck. I had nowhere in particular to go, insofar as I had all afternoon to write, and only wanted a few good words, maybe just 450 when I can easily write 4,500 in that amount of time. Four-hundred-fifty well-placed words, rather than 4,500 aimless ones, is better. I felt that I wasn't moving much, so I went for a walk instead.

Sometimes peoples' progress is imperceptible, or so slow it almost drives you crazy. Like a slowly moving river, their approach is wide rather than narrow, they aren't shooting through the rapids.

They wind around, rather than going in a straight line.

Their path is full of algae, even fallen branches, sometimes trash—shiny, empty skins of old Doritos bags, Pepsi cans sitting sideways their mouths half-filled with muck. They aren't moving fast enough to sweep the debris ahead of them. Sometimes it feels like they're even moving slower than they did before!

Are they getting anywhere at all? Does it even matter to them when the world around cries out with urgency?

I thought the river was in a conversation and it would turn out that the river was the listener today, but this is not the case.

Today, the river was the one being listened to. Nearly stuck, almost a pond.

But not quite. Gravity continued to gently play her part, softly drawing the river north, never screaming or begging for much motion; just a little, continuing the flow, and it would be enough.

When we're listening and hoping for progress, and inviting people to move, we must remember that an aqueduct such as the Pont du Gard has a drop of 34 centimeters over a kilometer; that the river in my town is only 801 feet above sea level and has plenty of time to get there with very little gradient.

Vitruvius, a first century civil engineer, recommended no more than a drop of 1:4800 for an aqueduct. That's because too much drop puts undue pressure on the system and causes more rapid deterioration of the entire system.

It's easy to panic when we think that there isn't time.

But there is time. Be a listener like gravity, a slow steady and constant pull. Even those drips who don't seem to be moving very fast will one day get to the ocean. Your interaction will be like 375 centimeter of drop in an aqueduct. Don't try to use gravity too fast; the system may degrade from pressure and erosion.

Figure 17. Moving slowly at the Mill Race in Goshen, IN.

When things move slowly (and you move beside them slowly), you'll see things a rushing river or a dead sprint might not give you: two turtles sunning on a log. Four ripe blackberries you can eat. A robin with a worm. When you move slowly alongside, you have the ability to avoid getting goose crap on your shoes. Slowly, you'll see a duck kicking her way upstream. "Don't paint her green," I reminded myself. Slowly, the river gets where it's going and you don't miss the scenery either. It's two for the price of one.

❖ What relationship do you have that's moving slowly?

❖ How can you match your pace to your friend's pace?

❖ How can you, like an aqueduct, lower yourself just enough to give the relationship a slight drop, drawing them toward the ocean like a slow river?

Listening to the blues
down on vortex street

No man is an island,
Entire of itself,
Every man is a piece of the continent,
A part of the main.
If a clod be washed away by the sea,
Europe is the less.
As well as if a promontory were.
As well as if a manor of thy friend's
Or of thine own were:
Any man's death diminishes me,
Because I am involved in mankind,
And therefore never send to know for whom the bell tolls;
It tolls for thee.[61]

—John Donne

For you always have the poor with you.[62]

—Jesus Christ

S ometimes life feels more like an ocean than a river. Tides slosh us back and forth, and the meteorological systems that accompany and impact our routines are far more complex. Then there's the foundational shifting of tectonic plates; in short, so many changes we can easily end up adrift.

On the heels of thinking about rivers that move so slowly, it's hard to tell they're going anywhere, or those lazy spots where everything's so wide it loses focus, I also see a place where things speed up so much they end up pushing us into reverse—the spin cycle, the eddy.

In an eddy, liquid spins backwards as it flows past an obstacle.

The old school language for this is backsliding, one step forward, two back, but the liquid in an eddy will eventually flow downhill with gravity, so this language feels more hopeful. That's easy when your life is like a river, but what about when mapping the complexity of your life feels more like oceanography?

Ocean vortices, also called mesoscale eddies, can sometimes last for months and cover areas as big as 500 kilometers in diameter. That's a really big spin.

Even more intriguing is the Kármán vortex street, a phenomenon when eddies in a repeating pattern happen on the backside of a blunt object, such as Mexico's Guadalupe Island, 150 miles west of Baja California. Guadalupe causes a vortex street almost every day from June to August. The eddies formed in a vortex street in the lee of an island take turns in a repeating pattern; imagine a repeating sine wave made of whirlpools.

The closer you are, the more likely you'll feel caught up in the vortex.

Obstacles that cause regular patterns in our lives can create surreal situations. Sometimes the obstacles in our lives are permanent and create vortex streets which become

Figure 18. Sketch of Kármán vortex street.

176

part of the landscape. Some days we can ignore them completely because we live with them; other days we have no choice but to acknowledge their existence and spend the entire day grappling with the problems they create.

I was talking to a friend of mine who routinely places in the top ten finishers in triathlons. He once qualified to participate in the US Amateur Triathlon. His fitness comes partly from an incredible work ethic and partly from a diet extremely low in fats because his body can't handle them. In fact, his pancreas rejects fats to such a degree that he's undergone multiple surgeries and has been in danger of losing his life. He schedules medical procedures so regularly, he says, "It's like the way you would schedule with your dentist or eye doctor." Who knows if he would still be surviving if he didn't push his body to the limit in training and competition whenever he's healthy? It gives him the ability to fight when his illness takes over for a period of time.

"It's surreal," he says, "I'll place sixth out of 200 racers in a triathlon, then I'll come home and there will be a medical bill I have to pay [from a procedure related to a chronic illness which has nearly killed him several times]."

The last time he was in the hospital, I went and sat with him for a couple hours, and I cried. I wonder when I will lose some of my closest friends who deal with diabetes or rheumatoid arthritis, and I treasure the small interactions of our lives; the sharing of a picture of their children on Facebook, a phone call to say "congratulations" for small victories, or "I'm glad you're feeling better today." I have my own health issues, and they do create a vortex street that exhaust me some days. But not as frequently.

Singing the blues is a simultaneous sharing of woes, while feeling good somehow that a better day will come. My friend Jonathan wrote a song that begins like this:

Better days gonna come again
put your raincoat on, you've been stuck in here too long.[63]

We have to get out. My friend who runs triathlons does this better than anyone I know. His body creates one of the most intense vortex streets you can imagine, but his discipline to get his raincoat on and get out to run in spite of the rain is an inspiration.

We usually feel like islands (and we feel that our own physical or emotional/mental selves are that obstacle which causes a vortex street) and yet John Donne insisted, we are not alone, that we must grieve every clod lost to the waves. When our friends are singing the blues on vortex street, our job is not to ignore, but to acknowledge, and to celebrate small victories as we navigate through the eddies. Perhaps worse than the backwards motion of backsliding, like a temporary eddy in a river, is the 300-mile wide mesoscale eddy in the ocean, or the vortex street that follows us around like a pair of ribbons streaming behind us, creating drag. The mesoscale eddy or the Kármán vortex street are disruptive, regular, and part of the ocean that picks away at our continent.

What's the motivational listener looking for? What's the value of recognizing a vortex street in a friend's life? We look for ways we find inspiration from their efforts and then highlight it. We invite people to get their raincoat on and get out. We see people in poverty create a symphony in spite of it (watch the documentary *Kinshasa Symphony* sometime). We see people in pain who compete in spite of it. We need to share each other's stories (with permission) and we need to be aware that some of us live with permanent obstacles and remind each other that we are not alone.

❖ Where can you spot people's disconnection to the mainland which is causing a vortex street? How can you help them remain connected?

When to risk it all

In coaching, we exercise discipline not to judge someone's actions. The classic training example is that your client wants to solve their money problems by buying a lottery ticket. Decisions you interfere with are all about potential results. But we can highlight three different levels of risk and ask about them: which type are you considering in your scenario?

Risk Type One: Zero Margin Catastrophic

Mistakes must be avoided at all costs. Cheating (cutting corners) is out. You cannot make a mistake when you face catastrophic danger. Once a year or so in my town, someone decides to go around a railroad crossing bar they think is malfunctioning, but it isn't and there is a tragic death. My policy is that you never, ever, under any circumstances, assume that the crossing bar is faulty. (After all, even if the gate is down and you've been sitting for a half hour without a train, that doesn't mean one isn't coming now. A busted clock is right twice a day.) If you allow it once and get away with it, you desensitize yourself and may be willing to do it again. You have to know if a shortcut could destroy you. If it could, don't go there.

Does your decision making have to be perfect (crossing train tracks, spacewalking)? Know when it does, and adjust.

Even if the odds are slim that you'll be wrong, what happens if you are?

Will it end in irreparable damage to something priceless (a relationship)?

Permanent cultural ostracism?

Premature death?

If the answer is, "Yes," you cannot afford a mistake. Your tail is not like a gecko's.

Your job as coach: spend all relational capital and confront.

Risk Type Two:

You can cheat towards your goal when you have a situational, calculated risk where the potential losses aren't catastrophic. They say that a base runner who is about to attempt a stolen base is "cheating towards second." If you are behind by five in the last inning, this is a stupid thing to do. If you are tied, it could be exactly the right thing to do. It's situational, strategic. If you lose, do you lose something that isn't really real (taking chances in a ball game, investing money, things you can afford to lose)? There may be times to take risks with your money. In other words, cheat your own system, bend your rules, rob from Peter to pay Paul for a while.

If there's a possibility you'll do real damage, are you willing to lose all your chips? Is it a good day to die? Are you taking a risk on a person who wants a shot?

Job as coach: help weigh chances, pros and cons.

Risk Type Three: Continual Growth Situation

Mistakes are inevitable, so proceed as usual. You cannot hold back when the opportunity is there for learning and growing. In a situation where perfection isn't attainable and the greater risk is that without moving forward you get farther and farther off track, it's better to make a small mistake, allow continual perspective from outside to shine light on your imperfection, and correct your course of action early (navigation, marriage, gaining an education/ taking a test in school).

Job as coach: support, encourage, give feedback.

Article 44

Do you drink the Kool-Aid ®?

I'm a pretty trusting guy. I grew up in a community called Plow Creek Fellowship, an intentional community church that was featured in *Newsweek* the same week they featured the Jonestown mass suicide when a whole ton of people committed suicide together by drinking poison-spiked fruit punch of some kind. The implication to have these stories back to back in the publication was the question: Is Plow Creek another doomed and dangerous cult?

Because of my background in communal living, I think twice when I hear people talking about "drinking the Kool-Aid."

It came up in some sales training I took a couple years ago. The idea the trainers presented was this: we have the best way to sell and if you buy in now and learn our process, you will be the better for it (rich). So buy-in immediately, don't bother with your skepticism if it seems "weird." Several times the trainers used the phrase, "Drink the Kool-Aid."[64] Really this isn't about it being weird or different than what you're used to. The underlying danger is that we

Figure 19. Kool-Aid is everywhere.

would stop worrying about what is *ethical.* But that's when our natural skepticism ought to rise up like bile within our throats and say, "Hold on a sec."

Why?

Because effective techniques (whether you're being trained in sales, leadership, coaching, ministry, business or being taught whatever else) ought to be self-evident to intelligent observers.

If you see something your trainer does that doesn't look like it would work on you, it probably won't work on other people either. (The problem is probably that it's being used ON people.)

On the other hand, when you see something that makes sense, just good ol' common sense, something you'd find attractive, a way you'd like to be treated, there's no Kool-Aid to drink; you're just in. We're not all killing ourselves for this thing, nor are we accepting anything but what's ethical and meets the golden rule. Dying to yourself isn't the same as drinking Kool-Aid. Drinking Kool-Aid has an implication of throwing common sense out the window and following a crazy leader into the abyss.

Dying to yourself doesn't mean throwing your life away in foolish pursuits. It means selecting the way to help others that makes the most sense to you, and giving up everything else.

❖ Where are you drinking the Kool-Aid? How can you die to yourself instead?

Article 45

Hearing God in the woods

If you go to the woods for a few hours to hear God and all you hear are songbirds, is that so much of a loss? And if you return home with reflections about songbirds which ring true, have you not then heard from God who is ever-expanding truth?

One of the greatest gifts you can give those you listen to is to spend time listening first to God, songbirds, and nothing in particular. Then you are (more) ready.

Spend five minutes praying without worrying about whether or not God has something to say to you—even if you don't believe in God at all. Tell God you are listening, and that it's OK if all you hear are birds or an air conditioner or someone sipping their coffee—even an annoying noise. Then ask:

❖ What do you like about who I'm becoming?

❖ Now take some notes: What did you hear? What was valuable about that?

❖ What did you not hear? What was valuable about that?

Article 46

Hedgerows

A human, of course, cannot speak with authority
on the motives of hawks. . . . The hawk came because of the con-
junction of the small pasture and its wooded borders. . . .
The human eye itself seems drawn to such margins,
hungry for the difference made in the countryside
by a hedgy fencerow.[65]
—Wendell Berry

Wendell Berry says we need to maintain healthy hedgerows where the wild meets the cultivated. Those hedgerows are places where foxes and hawks live, where biodiversity is maintained in favor of monoculture.

My wife does most of the gardening. Along the south side of our house, nearly invisible from the street, we have a variety of fruits and vegetables in a narrow strip. (We have a city plot so I'm talking about a strip south of the house between our foundation and the property line only six feet wide.) There are (failed) squash, tomatoes, rhubarb and raspberries this year. I know my veggies, but I'm always making up names for the flowers because I never know which name goes with which blossom.

"Look at these chrysanthemums, they're nice," I say.
"Those are peonies," she says.

"I like the daisies," I say, and she tells me they are lilies. I just found out this fall that mums are the same as chrysanthemums. Who knew you could nickname flowers? I shrug. Doesn't matter. Can't eat them.

But I do know what milkweed is; I've known it from childhood, and I've become more excited about it since reading Kingsolver's *Flight Behavior*.[66] I've allowed it to come up in a corner of my backyard, along this strip between the raspberries and the squash. That's because milkweed is the only plant on which the monarch butterfly will lay her eggs. It's called a weed, but the blossoms do have a sweet smell. Today, I was looking over the raspberries semi-productively, and suddenly, halfway through our second summer of allowing milkweed to stand in my mini-hedgerow, I got the reward: a monarch butterfly showed up and flitted about.

Making space for hedgerows is important to biodiversity, and when we strive to become better listeners, we also need to make space for an internal hedgerow. The analogy works two ways. First is the milkweed. I allowed it to grow in a space where we might plant a vegetable, something productive, or even a flower you might use in an arrangement; instead, milkweed in itself is not particularly beautiful and seems a waste of space. Some might say that for most of the year, it's even ugly. In fact, it's rather invasive and there's a real possibility I'll be overcome with them next year. That's like leaving space in your own life for time to create; the milkweed represents something a little more than the down time you have at the end of the day when you're watching television and there's no energy left, something that might even factor into your productive hours instead.

It's really hard to help someone make space for beauty to appear if you haven't practiced it yourself. We all know that we need breaks. But I'm not talking about five minutes. I'm talking about taking a half day to be "marginally" productive. This is not just a stupid pun. What I mean is that what we do during that time may or may not be useful later, certainly not in any obvious way. Taking time today to snap photos of "our" butterfly was that creative hedgerow time when it doesn't matter if anything really gets accomplished. This is one of the many photos of my first monarch.

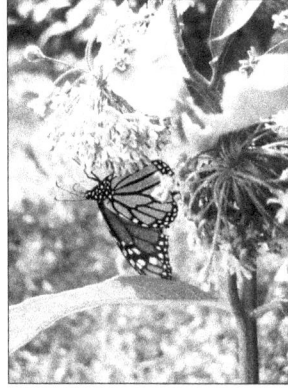

Figure 20. Monarch Butterfly. Status: near threatened.

The second aspect to the hedgerow is more like when the butterfly itself shows up, and it happens during a listening session. This is a conversational border area, a place (usually at the beginning and end) of a conversation where we aren't just cultivating our usual corn and beans that is, trying to be productive with our time. Instead we're just wandering through some hedgerow time together. The biodiversity in the hedgerow of a conversation can show us that wild side in our humanness. There's value in that wild side, beauty, moments of migratory musings and shy potential which can lead to the best stuff. It's why I prefer an hour session to a half hour when I coach. In 30 minutes, I can coach any issue beginning to end, but my client and I don't have the time for those extra moments to notice the best little pieces of life. Hedgerows have to be cultivated, too, but it's a cultivation of non-plowing, non-sowing. Make space for these kinds of margins in your week (allow milkweeds), and then in your conversation (be alert for butterflies).

We ended up seeing monarchs three or four times this summer. As far as I know, none of them laid their eggs on our milkweeds, but I'm glad to know the nectar sustained them. Perhaps next year some will begin to lay eggs, and we'll begin to see four and five at once.

Hedgerows II

W hen it comes to doing great listening I find that it's difficult to do without hedgerows. This term is a little like when people talk about having margins in their life, or perhaps somewhat like taking a regular Sabbath; but there's something more I want to explore with you.

Margins, of course, are neat and tidy. They are consistent. Whoever lays out this book will decide on a number, perhaps around five-eighths of an inch, and three-quarters in the gutter, so you don't feel the print is mashed up against the edge of the book. It gives everything a tidy feel, so that you have some breathing room. It's not wasted paper. It's paper used for nothing so you feel comfortable. When we talk about margins in life, we usually mean the time you take to get your coffee in the morning, watch a television show at night, or attend a festival with a friend on Friday night or Saturday. It's "Me" time, down time. Time spent NOT worrying about all the demands made on you by bosses, spouses, parents, children and even requests for your energy from places where you enjoy volunteering.

Sabbath is the last day of the week, the day of rest. Nancy Sleeth:

> "A recent poll of 2,000 pastors in North Carolina revealed that less than 10 percent are keeping a regular Sabbath. Think about this for a mo-

ment. If 90 percent of pastors announced from the pulpit that murder (or stealing, or adultery) is OK, don't you think it might raise a few eyebrows in the pews, let alone the press? ... decide what work is for you and don't do it on your Sabbath. For people engaged in sedentary work during the week, puttering around in the garden on the Sabbath might be restful. For people who do manual labor, holy rest might mean taking a nap."[67]

Sleeth's comment above points out that many of us, even (especially) pastors, aren't observing Sabbath.

OK. I don't know if you do or don't have margins on a daily basis or Sabbath weekly, but without them in first place, you can't grow a hedgerow.

Hedgerows are something different, something more than margins and a day off. Look up hedgerows on the Internet and you'll quickly realize that the most famous pop culture reference to a hedgerow is from Led Zeppelin's *Stairway to Heaven,* arguably one of the ten greatest rock anthems ever, in spite of the fact that nobody really knows what on earth this verse Robert Plant wrote actually means:

> "If there's a bustle in your hedgerow, don't be
>   alarmed now,
> It's just a spring clean for the May queen.
> Yes, there are two paths you can go by, but in the
>   long run
> There's still time to change the road you're on.
> And it makes me wonder."

Yeah ... it makes us all wonder. But that is the point—at least as far as my definition of *hedgerow* is concerned. It's a place to wander and wonder.

An actual hedgerow in England, where Robert Plant was familiar with them, is a stretch of semi-wild trees or shrubbery, (perhaps "with a path running down the middle—a path! A path!" as Monty Python's characters The Knights Who say Ni exclaimed) which creates borders between fields, a place where blackberries can grow, and children can disappear for the day and come home happy, dirty, and still wondering. It's right next to cultivated fields, so it's easily accessible from the places where you normally work, the places you keep much tidier and get what you expect. But spending any time tending and exploring the hedgerows only brings you surprises. A handful of edible mushrooms, priceless, not something you expected. Artists like Robert Plant and Monty Python seem to love their hedgerows, and give us unexpected things.

When I was a boy, we had a creek, woods, places to while away the summer days, unplugged. We could spend an afternoon exploring up the creek, farther each time, we could spend hours building a hut. The best hut was built after workmen with bulldozers cleared a field for a new blueberry patch. They pushed dozens of trees and brush up against the side of the field and into the woods, and on the back side, we found a hollow where the brush bent the trees over but did not knock them down. We took actual tools and bailer twine, spent hours building sides and a door, cutting and lashing, log cabin style, and camped out. We were so unplugged, so far away that we couldn't be called for dinner, or to take out the trash—and we liked it that way.

We never felt guilty about taking the time to do this. We saw it as a normal way to spend the day.

In the hedgerow, you may work, but it's a playful work. You may write an essay and decide it doesn't fit your book. You may run extra experiments for fun and discover something you weren't even researching.

I believe that a motivational listener needs to not only have margins and Sabbath but also must explore a hedgerow now and then. Perhaps even often. We gain perspective just by looking at the world differently. We follow a trail just to see where it goes; and if it goes nowhere, or to the dump where we might find some piece of junk we discover we need in our pocket, so much the better. When we're used to exploring hedgerows for ourselves, we're ready to guide others in that same quest.

When we listen, we listen for the interesting bits. Not only the parts where people are regularly cultivating a field. When I coach, the areas where my client has neatly plowed and planted, the parts of their lives that are in order, are not the places where we can discover anything new. We won't find the interesting rock walls to climb, the juicy blackberries to pick, and we won't spot a skunk in their neatly plowed fields. But if there's a bustle in the hedgerow, I follow it.

How do I schedule time to be in the hedgerow?

I can't tell you exactly how to loosen up your schedule. That's a problem for you on an individual level. (If you're having trouble doing it on your own, remember, you're a candidate for a wax job.) After all, it was somewhat forced on me by a variety of circumstances. One thing I can say for sure is that without it, I wouldn't be the motivational listener and storyteller that I am today, certainly not with the same quality and excellence.

I think this is something that business coaches often don't really find their way into. They move from high-powered executive positions to hard-charging coaches who are constantly selling, networking, and coaching, rarely with time themselves in the hedgerows. This makes it difficult for them to invite people into the hedgerow. For those of us in a busy Western world, or in a busy business environment generally (and they tell me now that things are even busier in Seoul and Singapore than they are in the USA). But business people don't need your help with more cultivation. They need help exploring hedgerows.

❖ How will I implement Sabbath and margins?

❖ What hedgerows will you explore?

Article 48

Getting my hedgerow time

I wouldn't have completed this book without significant time in the hedgerows. To and from my local coffeehouse, or the bank, I can walk instead of drive. Oftentimes when I walk to the coffeehouse to work on a manuscript or a blog, I arrive with better thoughts to write down quickly; instead of spending eight hours in a day typing, I have to get out and move for a while. In fact, after some hedgerow time, I find myself even *more* productive.

The thinking isn't done directly. My hedgerows, which are often just alleyways in a mid-sized Midwestern town, don't usually have blackberries or edible mushrooms growing. In one of his aphorisms, Taleb points out the irony of having a valet carry your suitcases to the hotel room, and later lifting weights in the hotel's exercise room.[68]

Like Taleb, I cannot see the value in paying for a gym membership. Supposedly they motivate you to work out more often since you've committed your dollars, but this doesn't always work for people and ends up being a profit center for the gym. Instead, I get paid to exercise and think—because when I walk I pick up aluminum cans. Perhaps I look as though I'm a bum, picking up others' trash, but there are several benefits to this method. First, of course I can cash in the cans after I accumulate quite a few, and this helps fund my non-profit's travel budget. Second, I beautify my city. Third, like blackberries or other delicacies one might hope to find, it gives me something to keep my eyes peeled for. There's something fun in finding that Coke or Coors can and scooping it into my bag. Plus, I learn about the drinking habits of people who litter unscrupulously (they drink Modelo by the railroad tracks).

In some ways, I'm combining exercise, thinking time (space I need to be able to be creative later), cleaning up my town, and there's even a little compensation for it.

The point is, you may not live in rural England with its beautiful hedges and idyllic scenery. Your town may be noisy, your streets may be dirty, but practicing *hedgerows* is really getting yourself in shape to *go to the edge of the world.*

They aren't the same thing. I think that, like Xi in *The Gods Must Be Crazy,* our walking may take us to the edge of the world. For Xi, a journey to the edge of the world, a journey of great discovery, started like mine does: when someone tosses a Coke bottle out the window.

When another character said they thought the end of the earth must be very far, Xi said, "I will start walking tomorrow."

It is much harder to find the edge of the world when we haven't been walking down the hedgerows. Xi couldn't have gone on his journey if he wasn't already quite conditioned for walking. Remember, the hedgerow is a space beyond your normal margins, beyond your normal day off. It's a call to seriously slow down, and to invite others to experience hedgerows as well.

❖ Will you start walking tomorrow?

Congo

One: A Brief History of a Forgotten Land
Charles Buller, my former pastor now with Africa Inter Mennonite Missions (AIMM), asked me to go to Kinshasa with him.

When I was a boy our family spent nearly a year in Congo, and I hadn't been there since 1988. For 27 long years, I'd been away from this land to which I thought I'd perhaps never return.

He said we'd go in August. Or September. Maybe October. I was OK with leaving it open-ended for a while, but, "I can't do November," I said. The idea was to do some very basic leadership coach training for Congolese Mennonite pastors, and I wanted to go. For a long time, it was up in the air. Eventually my tickets were for a departure from Chicago on September 3, 2015.

What does a leadership coach trainer have of value to take to the people of Kinshasa? Coaching is a key to options. Options are a key to infrastructure and an economic middle-class. An empowered middle class is a key to balanced leadership. Leadership is a key to the sustainable liberty of a people. And if anyone needs liberty....

The Portuguese took slaves from the coastal regions long ago, but Belgian King Leopold II's personal exploitation of Congo's interior was some of the worst treatment of people in the last 130 years. Mark Twain spoke out against it in his pamphlet "King Leopold's Soliloquy," a piece of political satire that set the stage for American comedic pundits like Jon Stewart. First-hand witnesses raised an outcry and ended Leopold's unrestrained theft. Leopold's pocket-lining set the example for the Belgians, then for Mobutu, who was Congo's kleptocratic dictator for over 30 years.

Maybe you've heard of Leopold, and Mobutu. But do you know the name Patrice Lumumba? Lumumba, the independent nation's first prime minister, was thought of as a great revolutionary, but he evolved into a volatile—if not completely out of control—leader once independence came to pass.

Lumumba met his end by firing squad. Mobutu, who helped kill him, set up memorials in his honor later to pacify the Lumumbist dissidents who didn't like his regime. In my boyhood, I visited Lumumba's birthplace, Onalua, with my brother. You won't find Onalua on Google Earth. Onalua is in the middle of nowhere. The monument was crumbling. We met a distant relative of Lumumba's. He was missing a leg, and he couldn't speak French. We went back to Wembo Nyama on our bicycles and that was the

Figure 21. *Left:* Author. *Right:* Brother, Aaron. In front of Lumumba's memorial, circa December, 1987.

end. It wasn't an epic adventure, but somehow I felt more tied to this country having seen the memorial of one of its greatest martyrs. Perhaps I felt that there were likely very few other Americans who had ever been to this spot, and I was a representative of some sort—a self-appointed ambassador.

After the cold war ended, when the USA needed much less uranium, Zaire was forgotten. Few Americans know where Congo is, who Mobutu was, fewer still, perhaps none but my brother and I, have been to Onalua to see Lumumba's proud, one-legged distant relative, who by now has almost surely passed away.

Two: Hopeful

Congo doesn't lack for spaces to grow food, catch fish; nor does it lack the natural resources needed for cottage industries. I'm not saying it's not poor—I'm just saying it doesn't need to be.

When I was in Thailand in March of 2015, talking with a couple missionaries, one said,

You will always have the poor with you.

and the other said,

Yes, but that doesn't mean they have to be hungry.

The idea to teach coaching principles in Congo is fraught with a variety of cultural pitfalls. One of the biggest challenges is translating a skill set for use by peers or equals into a society steeped in a tradition of hierarchical social structures. From the chief down; from the dictator down, from the bishop down, from the big boss down, everyone has to be very careful what they say to those above them, and to preserve their status, also to those below. Creating an atmosphere of authentic sharing even among spiritual brothers is a cultural challenge. Still, we hope that the ideas we can share in Kinshasa will give pastors a new paradigm, which leads to a new kind of accountability—one the leaders seek eagerly, rather than avoiding.

Yet even to say, "This is what we think you need," has an air of arrogance about it. I know Africa in general and Congo in particular needs leadership. But I approach the gift of training pastors there with a great deal of fear and trembling. It's humbling to be invited to provide something that holds out hope to such a hopeless place.

As we plan and prepare, I reflect more and more on the first experiences in Africa. I find my year in Zaire (Congo) 27 years ago the most difficult year of my life to write about. It's not that I'm shy about the psychological and social challenges I faced as a boy, the culture shock that was the bedrock of forming my identity in adolescence, it's just that this particular experience was so powerful. Perhaps it is the hopelessness that permeated it. I am not by nature hopeless. I will rise above the fears and doubts

Figure 22. *Left to right:* Aaron, Tom, Kay, Adam. *Front:* Bethany.

that drag me down, and so, I hope, will Africa, one day.

What hope did a man have to have so that he would journey 50 miles on foot with a silver French coin minted in 1853, saved who knows how many years in a secret place by people in his family, to bring this anachronistic remnant of colonialism all the way to Wembo Nyama to try to sell it at our house? Hoping that it may be worth some sort of fortune? And what happened to his hope when my father sent away to the States to determine an appropriate value, and the man waited three months for our correspondence to return, only to find out that the coin might retail at $10 in the States, and was generously offered the equivalent in rapidly devaluing zaires? He had to wonder if he was being robbed, as is practically traditional in an exchange between Congolese and westerners. He was offered for his antique French coin what was really a large sum in a country where people earned a dollar or two a month on average, but certainly no great fortune. A disappointment, that European silver. The hope is always bigger than the spendable cash you get for your prized possession.

What hope drove people to journey from the forest, knowing there were whites in Wembo Nyama, hoping we might buy monkey meat captured three days before and dangling in the 88-degree heat and 95 percent humidity from the back of their bicycle, an entourage of flies laying their eggs about the monkey's eyes, what disappointment when we didn't drop some cash, unburden them, take the microbiological risk on their protein-enriched delicacy? What disappointment for the hunter and forest-to-door salesman.

I will be delicate with you about the hopes of those with open wounds who traveled to our stoop hoping for a miracle cure, some medicine or perhaps a treatment. Mostly we had to turn people away. Living in Congo was an exercise in turning away the hopeful visitor.

There are no miracle cures today for Congo. There is not enough wealth we can offer for antiques or delicacies, and no amount of money or medical supplies that could heal this nation from the many ways it has been wronged, by Belgium, by the United States, by NATO, by big Chinese corporations, and even the leadership training we might provide this fall contains no miracle cure in itself. It must be applied. So how do we hold out hope that this thing is the thing, or even a thing? How will that help? But I am not by nature hopeless. If all we do is model a listening posture more than any westerner has exhibited there in 130 years, perhaps we can spark a revolution of listening. We can show what listening is by exceeding any expectations people may have for our listening.

Dream of a future with me where Congo leads central African nations to a new way of doing leadership that takes Africa back for the people. And when it happens, expect your cell phone to cost more because someone digging in eastern Congo is getting paid a living wage for the coltan in your electronics. They are so far removed, so forgotten, that we haven't even fathomed fair-trade electronics. Dream of great local leadership and fair-trade electronics at the same time. They go hand in hand.

Three: Memory and Art

A rain forest pins its own topsoil to the ground. Leave a slash-and-burn farming plot to its own devices for some time, just a year, and it will be overgrown. Things grow so easily in a rainforest, but what we love to call "improvements" are difficult to maintain. The rainforest forgets quickly.

Artwork, though, transports memory like a time capsule everyone can see all along, though they cannot imagine where it is going. Artwork moves through a generation without anyone noticing its sonder. Tribes co-create with much less thought to individual "intellectual property," with variations on a theme that may last hundreds of years, with craftsmen adding things in as they go. It is a mistake to think that any culture is static. In fact, memory plays a distinct role in how things stay the same, but it also impacts how things change. In cultures in which memories are traditionally handed down orally, the written word maintains a level of awe. So devalued is the written word now in the West that you expect to buy my next book for $0.99 or even get a free download, it is still a rare and important gift in Congo. The written word has powerful potential—and that power can be helpful or dangerous.

Charles and I talked about how we determine which coach training materials ought to be translated into French, and printed. This isn't easy. I'm concerned that any written "coaching question" may become a rote exercise rather than a flexible framework for conversation. I've seen it happen in "Life Transformation Groups" in the States, and I know that whatever we print will bear a certain inherent power.

I wonder if there's a way to mesh the coaching idea with the tribal approach to intellectual property—the idea that we create variations on a theme. Can the questions be developed as a masque is developed? (Not a mask as we think of wearing at Halloween.) I'm talking about a masque as something passed through initiation rites, an entire persona, costume and spirit together, something fluid from generation to the next, adaptable as new materials become available, but rooted in a tradition of authenticity and vulnerability rather than the traditions of secret societies? Yet moving into the future as a time machine? In context, there must be some certain rote steps to the dance, but room for creativity as well, like when an old masque costume is worn out and needs to be replaced, you see that suddenly the new one has Coke bottle caps attached.

As I consider this, I begin again to have faith that in Congo an approach to leadership, to coaching, and even to Christianity itself, can be contextualized by those who know themselves—by the Congolese. A mix of tradition, rote learning, dance steps that stay the same, building a framework for love, for authentic relationship, can emerge, and can be remembered powerfully, in a good way.

We want to bear faith to Congo that we believe the Congolese can integrate and contextualize coaching to help them take off masks that need to be removed, but that the idea of a masque-like conversation as a ritual dance for the community can be useful and transformational.

Four: Falling out of the sky

David Law flew me back to Wembo Nyama. I was 14 and had spent four weeks away from my family. I needed a break from them, and everyone knew it.

The last straw was the night I smacked my little sister with a steel bowl, right on top of her head. At five, she was prone to running about naked, which embarrassed me, especially since we lived in a fish bowl. I mean that, at night, in one of the few houses with electric lights, it was not unusual to realize that neighborhood children's eyes were peering in the windows. They were only children, naturally curious, wondering what these whites did at night in their closed-door, brick and tin-roof oven of a house. Seeing my sister, the nudist, in all her blonde Caucasian glory. As if we needed more reason for people to gawk. I was embarrassed, angry, peerless and alone, culture-shocked, stressed, dealing with my sister's exhibitionism so my concern about the "paparazzi" was too much to bear, and I thumped her with a bowl and it sounded like a gong. And of course, she cried quite a bit.

So they sent me to stay with the Laws for a while. A half-hour flight or so in a single-prop Cessna to a different mission station. Take a break. Grow up a bit. Get some perspective. Stop fighting with dad. Socialize with some other Westerners. I would put on my sneakers and go for hour-long runs on the savanna where I could focus on my breathing and watch the occasional dung-beetle who also had to deal with his crap every day, as he rolled his treasures across the same dry plateau; it was a chance to think only about as much as the beetle was thinking. *Bring it home, just find a way to get it home.* I fell in love with running. It was one foot in front of the other, thoughtfulness without the need for a specific idea. General Awareness. You got your second wind, found your pace, and coasted along the dirt track in silence and slid back into the house unnoticed, sweating out any toxic anxieties in the process.

Before I went to stay with the Laws, I was going a little bit nuts, maybe a bit beyond the tolerances of normal adolescence. "Maybe," I say, because even in retrospect, I realize that I only grew up once, and it happened to be in the middle of Zaire. So how would I know for sure if I was beyond my own ability to cope with being 14 in any way worse than it might have been in Illinois on a strawberry farm where I knew the difference between fruit and weeds? But I'm pretty sure the added stress meant I was not coping as well as I might have in the States. I was psychologically taxed.

At the end of my retreat, as we flew back into Wembo Nyama, David said over the noise of the engine, "Check this out. I can cut the engine and we can glide the last two miles to the strip. Nobody will hear us coming." Usually the arrival of an airplane was a major deal. Hundreds of people would show up at the strip to gawk at the plane, welcome strangers or say goodbye, help out with luggage somehow, hoping for a tip. To surprise my parents by walking in the door without anyone in town noticing, I liked this idea very much.

He cut the engine and turned the Cessna into a hang glider. The wings would bear us up just long enough to reach the strip and coast to the end. We began to lose altitude. I might have been afraid we'd crash, but my pilot was confident. It occurs to me now that because David's father

Figure 23. Congo savanna viewed from the air, 1987–88.

was shot upon landing at Wembo Nyama in '64, I wonder if he was somehow paying tribute still in '88. [A moment of silence for

Burleigh Law, missionary pilot and martyr.] The air rushed by, our velocity kept us moving forward, and all was still.

I had gone from the middle of nowhere to the edge of the world. For a moment I had the satisfaction of peace, of nobody knowing where I was, hanging in the air like a soul suspended in an out-of-body experience, not sure whether to live or die, looking down upon myself under some sort of anesthesia, and being really good with that. That's the way I'd felt when running on the savanna too, me and the dung-beetle paying obeisance to the hedgerow concept. Nobody knew where we were, and we just bore our crap onward one step at a time and picked up on the little things that didn't matter and somehow in the not-mattering, they mattered. Life is made of matter and so much more, and so it matters.

A half-dozen aviation enthusiasts noticed us coming, but there wasn't the usual dozen-times-a-dozen spectators as we rolled down the last bit of clay airstrip, touching down like an ace at Wimbledon in that hush of the serve. I really did surprise my parents when I walked in the door.

It's significant for a person like me, who likes the bright lights of a stage, to have that desire to walk unnoticed. Coasting in that Cessna, in silence through the air currents on the outskirts of Wembo taught me that the ability to be at peace, and, at the same time, to be unnoticed while falling out of the sky, is a valuable art. That's what I like about the riskiness of coaching someone. I can turn off the engine that drives my own decision-making process and let the wings of listening interact with the air of my client's living and breathing and let them land on their own runway—or take off for jungles and oceans, all hopes for success, so long as they push their own crap down the path before them.

Five: Perspective

Like many third-culture kids, I love to fly. You're going some-where, you're in transition, and you're getting new perspective all the time.

David Law, whose father Burleigh was martyred in Wembo Nyama in the late 1960s when he flew in to evacuate other mis-sionaries and was unable to beat the rebels into town and was shot by one of them when he landed, liked to use his airplane as a hot air balloon sometimes and as a race car other times.

On one trip, he flew at an altitude above the savannah of about 60 feet. It felt like 10 feet. It was high enough to clear the short savannah trees and taller termite hills, but low enough that the grasslands went by at a high speed blur, 120 to 150 miles per hour. I am not sure if this was a particularly safe way to travel, or whether it was safer than flying higher if you had engine trouble, for example, or whether it was less safe.

I didn't think about safety. I just enjoyed the race car per-spective, skimming along like that.

The higher you fly, the more you feel that you aren't going anywhere. In a huge airliner on a 14-hour flight when you get to that 5 or 6 mile high altitude, even if you look down, and can see the ground, it doesn't feel like you're really getting anywhere. You're also very likely to not see anything at all—the cloud cover prevents you from seeing land, ocean or glacier. I saw the glaci-ers of Greenland once; you also don't think about safety when you're riding that high. If you go down, your odds are not good. Why don't they put in a comfortable seat instead of an upside down life jacket? If you need the life jacket, you probably don't, and if you don't, then why not have a comfortable ride? Unless your pilot is used to flying gliders like the man who landed a just-lifted-off plane in the Hudson River after leaving LaGuardia, you are going to be comfortable until you're dead.

Perspective is all about altitude. It's been said that nobody uses a five-year business plan anymore. Things change too quickly. You can make a five-year plan, but you really can't see much from five miles high, it's too cloudy and you don't feel like you're moving.

On the other hand, if you fly too low, you're met with a rush of detail you can't really absorb.

The perspective I like is a mid-range perspective. I like that phase of flight when you're low enough to see some of the ground. I love to fly at night over the Midwest in the summer. You see the baseball diamonds lit up in groupings like four-leafed clovers and you can pick out the towns. When you come into Chicago, you get a clear distinction between the city and the lake it spoons. I love to fly at a mid-altitude level where the ground is moving along, but you can at least guess: coming from Atlanta to South Bend, first I spot maybe Knoxville, now we're over Louisville, then Terre Haute, we bank over Notre Dame's golden dome and land.

We need to ask for the level of detail we want to hear—the level from which we can have a useful perspective. This isn't to say we shouldn't ask now and then where you'd like to be in 10 years, or that the focus couldn't be on the four decisions we have to make next week. The urgent decisions of turning have to blend with the longer-range relevancy of direction.

I used to use the metaphor "find true north" for my business motto. I still like it. Our primary instrument for navigation in the northern hemisphere has always been Polaris. It's interesting that what flies over us at a much greater altitude than five miles can give us much more pinpointed location when we feel lost than any amount of tree-climbing to try to see what's around us could ever do, if we know how to access it. But Polaris is a metaphor for the Creator—something that seems distant at times but is so intimately associated with direction that it can always tell us exactly where we are.

Since I'm not the Creator and can't fly as high as Polaris, my choice is to fly at some sort of middling altitude if I want to be at my most useful.

❖ Are you looking up to Polaris, or are you looking down to identify landmarks and landing strips? Neither is bad. Both are helpful. But be aware of which direction you need to look to get your bearings.

Article 50

Congo and the good guy

W e don't get much news about events going on around
the world when nobody knows who the good guy is.

One of the main arguments people have against
pacifism is the standard, "What about Hitler? How can you say he
shouldn't have been stopped?" question. The question is never
posed in reverse, though, such as, "What about Johnson & Nixon's
bombing of Laos?" Shouldn't they have been stopped? But this is
the camp known as "us" and so for as long as we assume that we
are the good guys, we cannot see the ethical dilemma this question creates.

To the victor goes the spoils, and perhaps one of the most
important spoils is the power to write history textbooks. But
muddying the waters are those times when it's really hard to tell
who the bad guy is. Then, we just don't get any information at all.

> "The Second Congo War disappeared from
> the international media reports because it was
> considered incomprehensible and obscure. And
> indeed, there were no two clearly delineated
> camps; even more, there was no clear division of
> roles into villain and underdog. After the Cold
> War, Western journalists increasingly came to
> apply a moral frame of reference in reporting on
> armed conflicts: in Yugoslavia, the Serbs were the

major culprits; in Rwanda, the Tutsis were the innocent victims. In both cases that led to disastrous misrepresentations and policy measures. In Congo it was not particularly easy to find a 'good' side. Anyone viewing the conflict from close up knew that all those involved had their own skeletons in the closet. The grievances often seemed justified and the methods chosen often problematic."[69]

When journalists start having trouble putting people into "good" and "bad" camps, they stop covering issues. Like an addiction to refined sugar, we want polarization in our news diet. There's no room for the bitterness of an ambiguous but honest report, and we reject it like a sugar addict rejects a kale smoothie.

❖ Find sources for information that don't assume one answer. Find sources for people who can support you who also don't assume there's only one answer. How can you become this kind of support to others?

Article 51

Motivation

D an Pink did a great job on the makeup of Motivation in his book *Drive.*[70] Here's perhaps an incomplete list of things we may need motivation FOR:

- ➢ Pushing ourselves to greater excellence
- ➢ Pushing the limits of our endurance
- ➢ Getting through unpalatable tasks
- ➢ Taking risks
- ➢ Making new habits out of aspired values

These are the things to listen for and support.

❖ What do you need motivation for? If you think of anything that doesn't fit within one of the five ideas above, email me! Ask others which of these five things they have the most trouble getting motivated to do, and support that with encouragement and accountability.

Truth

There are glimpses of truth in a butterfly, in a novel, in a crumbling building, in a child's request for a peanut butter sandwich—or just about anything else a child says (even when lying, there's a deeper truth: What are they afraid of?).

Listen for truth, you won't be disappointed. The world is full of it.

❖ Where can you look for truth that you haven't looked before?

Article 53

Pontius Pilate

Answers are sought for self-preservation. You must be willing to die for truth.

"What is truth?"[71] Pontius Pilate asked. For eternity the Bible will record that Jesus gave him no verbal answer. Jesus wasn't into answering people's questions for them. Jesus never said He was The answer. He told His disciples that He was the truth. Whether you believe this about Jesus or not, imagine yourself confronted with universal truth embodied. Your options are simple. Recognize and embrace it even if it means your death, or ignore it.

Judaea was not an easy place. One might say that the Roman prefect was stuck between a Rock and a hard place. Perhaps to annoy the Jews who had aggressively played him, he acknowledged Jesus when he wrote Jesus' reason for conviction as "King of the Jews," not as "*he claimed* he was the King of the Jews." But could this not be because Pilate respected Jesus' refusal to play games? Moreover, did Pilate not see exactly this: that while Pilate needed some sort of answer to preserve himself as prefect, to preserve Pax Romana, his highest goal and expectation, he saw that Jesus was willing to eschew answers in favor of dying for, because of, and as the truth? Pilate seems to have sensed that Jesus had given His own power up into Pilate's hands, if only by refusing to play political games.

Pilate could have said, "No." He could have listened to his wife. There are a variety of ideas about what happened to Pilate later, but according to some reports, Pilate committed suicide sometime around 37 or 38 AD, perhaps no more than five years after giving Jesus up to crucifixion. Do you blame him for wanting an answer? I don't.

Pilate was not given cultural sensitivity training by the HR staff in Rome before he was sent to Caesarea in AD 26. He lasted 10 years by shrewdly avoiding absolute truths in favor of decisions intended to preserve his position.

Like Jesus, motivational listeners die to themselves for the sake of seeking truth. Instead of offering answers from the void between our ears, we ask questions. Like Jesus in the garden of Gethsemane we lay our agenda down, willing to die for truth.

So what's wrong with answers? When we decide we've got the world figured out, we can A) dismiss anyone who doesn't believe we have THE answer, B) place ourselves in the center of the camp of those who think rightly about things. These approaches both isolate us from others who are searching for truth so that the more we hold that answer-torch high as statues of liberty so often want to do, fewer are the people who harbor in our shores. Like the boys in *The Lord of the Flies,* it looks more like we've set our island on fire. We thought we were smoking out the dangerous lone wolf of that which is yet unknown; instead we destroy our entire ecosystem, making it uninhabitable for ourselves and for anyone who might come along later. The flames of our overzealous desire to hold all the cards end up being the biggest distress signal ever seen.

The first step is to admit frequently that we don't have the world figured out. The funny thing is that the common perception in pop culture right now is that "the Life Coach has it All Figured Out." Nothing could be more misleading! Instead, while asking good questions the asker must remain flexible. When we work on a SMART goal, the key is that the goal must be relevant to your values. The thing about values is that they aren't static. Being open to truth means being open to answers—that is, decisions about how to live—that are constantly open to reflection upon new aspects of truth being brought to light. This is why a good listener is willing to allow the client grace as things develop. It's been said that no poem is ever finished, only abandoned. Does this mean there is no answer—no perfect poem? Yes. The poem gets worked on until the relevance of perfecting it decreases enough for the poet to jump ship and look for a new island of emotion to attempt to express.

Answers are for self-preservation. Questions leave you vulnerable. But you must be willing to die for truth.

My sympathy goes out to Pilate. He lived in a nation more politically polarized than the United States in our day, a time and place where people post hatred of government officials and candidates on Facebook as casually as they post pictures of what they're eating.

Like any Roman official who survived in any corner of the Empire, Pilate sought answers (allowing for a decision on how to act or proceed) for the challenges his office brought him, challenges that were not only culturally confusing for him, but where every decision meant a riot could break out at any moment. The wrong move meant a disgraceful departure from office at best, execution for his entire family at worst. The stakes were high for Pontius Pilate to find the right answers every time, in every situation. In an earlier article, I discussed the idea that truth is both expanding and contracting (an idea of mine which may well be wrong). Assuming it has some merit, then, to the extent that truth is contracting (becoming more limited and narrower each day) we must cling tightly. But in ways that truth is expansive, we can hold on loosely, so that when we take action, when we take a paintbrush to paper, swing at the ball, or attempt to connect in any other way, our action will indeed produce the results we're hoping for.

❖ How will you act or proceed the next time you're talking with someone who is wrong? How will the conversation change when you hold more loosely to the truth?

❖ Where must you draw the line as truth contracts?

Was Judas Iscariot a
leadership guru?

W hen I train businessmen in basic coaching skills, the question of building leaders the hard way by allowing them to fail, often comes up. "What if I let someone make their own decision and it hurts the company? We lose a major client? We lose money? All because I let them make a decision?"

First of all, leadership is in many ways about decision making. C-level people are paid what they're paid not because they know how to run a website effectively, how to do bookkeeping, etc. They're paid to make strong decisions. It follows that leadership development, or coaching young leaders to take increased roles in leadership, will necessarily mean asking them to make decisions that are perhaps over their heads at the moment. This leads to an unusually high level of mistakes. The biggest decision the C-level person has to make is deciding who to invest in as the next leader. Pick someone of character, then make sure you have the margin so they can fail when they make decisions and you'll all survive their development stage. Well ... maybe. I can't guarantee it. But it's still the best way to develop the next generation.

When I get into reading about Judas, I envision a guy who probably thought he was the most legitimate right-hand guy for Jesus when he came into His kingdom. It's been speculated that the guys who really did ask for this (pressured by their mothers, of all people) were somehow related to Jesus. In an oligarchy-prone society, that would make sense. But Judas probably saw that there was more of a meritocracy going on. A weird one in which you don't ask if you get to be first in line. So he didn't. Besides, Judas was a cool dude. Not a country rube blurting out stuff like, "Hey, can I sit at your right hand??" A real rebel, a tough, action-based leader, looking for—and finding—the real Messiah, and aligning himself in the right camp. He was the bookkeeper. A high-trust position. Maybe it should have gone to a guy like Matthew, but it didn't. Jesus picked Judas because he was in Jesus' special leadership training track. At least I imagine this is what Judas thought. I suspect that's what Jesus hoped for too.

This is where people begin to question my thinking, and rightfully so. I want to state right up front that it's possible my interpretation (really just a speculation) is completely false. The question is: Wasn't Judas's entire life lived for the express purpose of betraying Jesus? But my concept in this article is developed based on the overall tone of the gospels, where Jesus is a *consistent* developer of leaders. He knew what Judas would do (though we are not told when Jesus became conscious of this) even while he hoped for something better for Judas. He seems genuinely surprised when Judas does it with a kiss. "Do you betray me *with a kiss?*" [emphasis mine]. Certainly Jesus, who knew people's hearts and thoughts was not above being surprised by the depths to which we can stoop. Before I continue I want to acknowledge the paradox I'm working with here. There's an idea here about Judas that is so unorthodox it may be uncomfortable. I think there's something in the nature of God worth exploring in this way of looking at the end of Judas Iscariot as a leadership guru. Let's assume for the sake of this discussion that Jesus knew what would happen based on peoples' hearts, but could also be surprised. This is really the first paradox: that an omniscient being could be surprised. (I suspect that He was just as surprised by the faith of a Roman centurion who asked Jesus to heal his servant at a distance as He was by Judas coming to betray Him with a kiss.)

Back to Judas. Everyone is in awe of Jesus stilling the waves, healing the sick, and perhaps most of all, knowing what they are thinking. That is freaky stuff. Have you ever had someone know what you're thinking? Maybe a spouse after at least 10 years, but your CEO, after two or three years? Not just knowing sort of what you're thinking, knowing EXACTLY what you're thinking. Freaky for most. But Judas wasn't surprised by that. Judas expected the Messiah to show up with some considerable superpowers. Expectations met. Check, check, check. When Jesus said, "What you are going to do, do quickly,"[72] look at it from the perspective of someone who's constantly developing leaders to think for themselves, and then see the perspective of the man who is being developed. The message as Judas reads it is this: "You're the number one sidekick tonight. I know what you're thinking about doing, Judas, and we're on the same page. You've formulated a plan, and it's a good one, because it will catalyze the kingdom, and we need you to take your action step." Judas thinks, "Peter talks big, James and John thought they were in tight, but I'm a man who takes action." I'm confident that Judas thought of himself as a catalyzing leader. If you were getting coached by Jesus into a right-hand-man leadership position, and He told you to plan your work and work your plan, isn't this what you'd assume Jesus means by such a statement?

The best argument I have for these assumptions is that Yahweh isn't a Father who uses people. A key leadership coaching principle is that you *use tasks to build leaders, not leaders*

to accomplish tasks. This principle is consistent Yahweh-behavior from Joseph, Moses, Joshua, Gideon, Saul, David, Nehemiah, right down through. Why would it change for Judas? Judas is often held up as perhaps the greatest example of predestination: under that thinking, Judas was made for this moment, like a card you pick up in a game specifically because you know you're going to need a discard later, something to trash. Jesus knew his Abba God *don't make trash,* and He don't use or treat people like trash, so I speculate that an alternate possibility is that Judas really WAS on a special leadership track. None of the leadership development stuff God consistently did with all other biblical leaders makes sense if He ditches the methodology when He gets to Judas. At least, at some level, I do think that Judas was chosen as an apostle because Jesus saw some spark of a potential leader in him. The idea that Jesus hit 11 for 12 is not an indicator of Jesus' failure (oops, He got one wrong, guess He wasn't perfect after all). No. I think in the part of Jesus' mind that could be surprised by human behavior, there must have been days when He thought to Himself, "Did I go 0 for 12 when I picked my lineup?" Looking at it this way, the ultimate success rate of 11 for 12 is pretty good because it's all based on **leaders taking responsibility for their own lives**. If you could get 11 out of 12 of your leaders to take responsibility for the work after you leave your company or church or nonprofit, wouldn't that be pretty fantastic? After all, that's not your choice to make. But you can *HOPE.*

Jesus hoped they would all be such great leaders that He was willing to lay down His own life. Look, the Pharisees were going to get to Jesus one way or another. They'd been plotting to nail Him, and it was a matter of when. Jesus encouraged Judas to take the action step as a means of *allowing* him to be part of the inevitable process, not as a means of *forcing* him. (Of course, several gospels also note that Satan, or the adversarial spirit, had entered into him, and that's the part of the paradox I'm not addressing.) Let me say this again: God didn't NEED Judas to do this, I speculate and strongly suggest God didn't CREATE Judas to do this. He ALLOWED Judas to do it as a part of His leadership development plan. It was anticipated that Judas would realize it as a mistake, yes, but is it possible that the Father and Son both always hoped that he would live and grow through it, to become one of the most powerfully humble leaders the Way would perhaps ever know? A hope against all hope, against all omniscience, a hope that Judas would surprise them? Peter chickened out and denied Jesus; he became the leader of the church. Judas did even worse, so by the same token, he might have done even more. This is because the power of the message of redemption is in direct correlation to the former depths of betrayal.

I am happy to say that I am not certain we can make a doctrinal statement here. However, I am confident enough in my observation that this controversial reading of Judas is consistent with how Jesus did leadership development, and I recognize that I'm mostly exploring the side of the whole Judas-predestination paradox (Satan enters him, but he makes his own decisions too; Jesus knows what he's going to do; it's inevitable, but still surprises Jesus) which has more to do with what Jesus might have hoped for all His disciples—namely, that after the chaos of crucifixion, they'd all find their way back to the group, and become the church.

I have a strong suspicion that Jesus was always more hopeful for how the life of Judas could turn out than we've ever imagined. It gives me comfort to think that He'd have such an attitude, a hope for me whenever I turn out to be one of the bad guys, as well. I hope that sharing this idea would give you hope, too. I have wrestled with this idea for several months, realizing that it's the most controversial idea in the entire book. I also feel that the theme of the entire book leads us up to this idea: we know a lot less than we think we do; we have a lot more choice than we think we do; we can surprise God; God hopes for our success even as He foresees our failures; Jesus continues to listen, to present Himself as the Question. "Instead he is patient with you, not wanting anyone to perish, but everyone to come to repentance."[73]

When we talk about laying down our lives for the people we lead or coach, whether in our business or in our church, this includes encouraging them to take action steps that may even hurt us. We may lose money. Our church may split. Rough years ahead while they fumble their way through their new, perhaps even premature, leadership opportunity. It's potentially death for you to let a young leader make decisions. But it's the only way they can learn—truly learn to be a leader. I grieve the loss of Judas. If he'd stuck around just one more day—two more days—we might have a "Book of Judas" somewhere in the Bible. If we did, it would probably be a book about action and decision making and financial stewardship "God's Way"—it would have been the book that preceded a LOT of the leadership books on your shelf right now—perhaps even making the en-masse writing of all those other leadership books already a moot point; a leadership message embodied in the life of Judas that had to be discussed by committee instead. Or it might not have been written, because Judas may have been such a man of action that he would not have had time to stop and write anything down. Who knows? (That's kind of the point: who knows?)

But I submit that his impact could have been huge, standing next to Peter at Pentecost. Travelling with Paul or Timothy or Barnabas, or staying in Jerusalem to zealously evangelize the Jews. Perhaps the impact of his life might have meant more unity between Jewish and Gentile congregations in the first century, or between the Roman and Greek churches hundreds of years later. More unity between Rome and the Protestants. Less crusading. Who knows, who knows? His actions for the rest of his life might have been an impact that his replacement never made—not to say that Matthias didn't make an impact. (I say this because I know Judas is a household name, even outside of the Christian faithful, and Matthias is not.) Who knows how having Judas for a few more precious years, after what he'd learned in the crucible of Jesus' leadership training program, what that might have done for all of us? Though Judas may have been destined to be a suicide, a discard, a complete loss, I propose that Jesus hoped he would instead become a leadership guru. Our loss.

- ❖ Whose mistakes are you shying away from right now because you don't think they are ready?

- ❖ What leaders have you asked to fulfill already-determined actions, rather than inviting them into the decision-making process itself?

- ❖ How can you give greater responsibility to someone knowing they may fail? What margin do you need to grow so that you can do this more? What are you willing to lose?

- ❖ What potential betrayal could you dare to stomach? Where can you send your young leader to interact with other leaders—where they might end up leaving your sphere and following—eventually leading elsewhere, in spite of your investment?

❖ Which of these questions need to be asked in your context in a less vague, more specific way? How would you make them more specific?

Article 55

Sentinels of isolation

P art of doing great accountability is helping people avoid the dangers of isolation. When we're isolated, we can't really progress. Now, I'll be the first to say that too much progress is not necessarily a good thing. But when we're truly isolated, not only are we prone to flawed-character activity (i.e., sin) but we also can't really learn anything new from others. Anything from technology to language. We cease to communicate, and we end up like the Sentinelese. I became fascinated by the Sentinelese culture and spent an entire evening reading everything there is on the Internet. Which isn't much. Because they're very isolated. So that's the point.

North Sentinel Island in the Andaman Island chain contains the greatest example of an isolated culture left on the face of the earth. Numbering somewhere between 50 and 400, the inhabitants are locked in Stone Age life; it's unclear whether they're capable of using fire; their weapon of choice is a bow and arrow or spear which they might be tipping with metal from shipwrecks. When intruders come for a visit, the good Sentinelese people kill them. The Indian government, which recognizes them as essentially sovereign, understands their position to be one of self-defense. The last time they killed some poaching fishermen, the Indian government did nothing. As near as I can tell, there has only been one exception to this rule of violence, when a group of anthropologists from India took gifts of coconut and came very close to shore.

The Indian government's official policy is that nobody is allowed to contact the Sentinelese. For one thing, nobody can speak their language. You're likely to be killed; in one image from the Indian Coast Guard, a Sentinel islander on the beach dares a helicopter to land by drawing his bow and aiming skyward. The pilot decided against it.

Figure 24. Sentinelese.

And if you did go there, you'd be likely to kill them by spreading infectious diseases the Sentinelese are unable to combat; their immune systems can't take it.

It is incredible to me that these people have had such little contact with the outside world for 5,000 years minimum. Some scientists think they've been alone on North Sentinel for 60,000 years.

I think it's easy to idealize this primitive life. For one thing, these folks are so in tune with their natural surroundings, they appeared unharmed and unfazed when the tsunami destroyed so much in 2004. It is speculated that the Sentinelese were tipped off to the coming tsunami by something they alone would see and know in the waves that lap their shores. (The helicopter which took the picture I mentioned was there to check and see if they were OK after the tsunami.) So the signs they read from the waves and sky, the fish and trees, has a vocabulary for "here comes a tsunami, head to higher ground." On the flip side, it's also easy to idealize our technology-heavy culture. We have ships and helicopters. We must seem to them as though aliens from another world had come to visit, perhaps to abduct them for horrible scientific procedures. Or perhaps we seem like demons. In any case, our technology doesn't protect us from tsunamis.

Two takeaways: the most notable thing is not whether living the Stone-Age *vida loca* is some sort of paradise on earth without knowledge of kindling, or whether these folks would be better off reading my book on their Kindles. The most notable thing is their fear. Whatever else isolation has given them or taken away, they are afraid. Always afraid. Afraid in every recorded encounter. Isolation breeds fear. Secondly, when we're isolated for too long, we don't have immunity to things as we ought. When we're surrounded by diversity, yes, we might contract a nasty disease, but we also have the ability to build immunities through frequent contact with other humans. It doesn't mean we can't get sick. In fact, we're more likely to catch a cold. But it also means that others will be able to help us if we stay connected.

❖ How will you stay connected to your community?

Embracing the stuntman

This is a dialog with Benjamin Baker. Benjamin is a 2015 Foundational Coaching Skills trainee, and I consider him a good friend.

Adam:

We've talked a lot about authenticity and vulnerability, and your own journey towards living those things out. You had some really interesting ideas about this idea you call the "grey man" and the contrasting "stuntman." How would you define these two characters?

Benjamin:

The grey man is just a way of describing someone who doesn't stand out, they blend in so well in a crowd or life that they're practically invisible. Not to say that they're truly invisible, but when you think back to a time or situation, that's when they disappear.

And the stuntman, well, let's just say he's the opposite of the grey man. When referring to professional stuntmen, whether we're talking about the guy jumping over cars and stuff on a motorcycle, or the guy driving a car that explodes for a scene in a movie, those both demand our attention and aren't doing things to disappear, blend in, or be unseen. Living with the stuntman mentality is about not hiding. It's about embracing your fear with bravery, boldly facing the scary and being vulnerable.

Adam:

There's something about owning it when you do something crazy that people actually rally around, and though some will be haters, you can really get some mileage out of being a stuntman. When I posted this picture to Facebook for the first time after my son Timothy and I put it together, the first comment I got was, "I love your confidence." You do have to own it, but even if it looks fantastic doesn't mean that going after a dream or just being you, publicly, is an escape. In fact, it's a

Figure 25. The author as a "stuntman." Photoshopped by his son Timothy.

more real version of yourself than most people are willing to project to the world. You're not escaping life, you're embracing it. We talked about some real practical things having to do with escapism, like eating all your meals in front of the television. In contrast, you talk about embracism, the idea that you face things rather than hide from them. What's embracism all about?

Benjamin:

Embracism is the cold shower of life. It defies the comfort zones. What I mean is that warm showers are nice, but there are real

Figure 26. Benjamin Scott Baker. Stuntman extraordinaire.

benefits to taking cold showers. But you have to be bold enough to do it. When taking a cold shower, you just dive in and own it. Embrace the fact it is going to be very uncomfortable at first, but you'll survive and in the end, reap the benefits of it. That's kind of like this embracism. Not everyone will do it either, some only want the escaping comfort of metaphoric warm showers.

According to a persuasive Internet meme I saw once, "Life begins at the end of your comfort zone, man...." (OK, so I added the "man...." but I thought it worked well there). Instead of holding tight to your comfort, it's going ahead and pursuing what makes you uncomfortable for a minute, to achieve what you really want in the end, man.

Adam:

You mention that you're good at low-risk disciplines (like disciplining yourself to a healthy diet) but you know that you shy away from disciplines that might lead to the kind of success that puts you on other peoples' radar. I'm pretty interested in risk taking. We talked about radio personalities and bloggers who constantly come under fire, censor their own critics and then defend themselves—and what a turn-off that is. What's the alternative to defending yourself once you've taken those steps that put you in the unenviable position of being attacked for no good reason (like, virtually anything and any way that you could possibly be vulnerable on the Internet)?

Benjamin:

Winston Churchill once said, "You have enemies? Good. That means you've stood up for something, sometime in your life."

If you stand for anything at all, someone will be upset with you; it's going to happen. When I was a kid, I was never that great at skateboarding because I couldn't deal with the fact that I was going to fall and I was going to get hurt. There's no way around it if you want to be really good.

You can form your ideas and opinions all day long, which is just as important as learning how to move and stay balanced on a skateboard. But once you actually stand for something, that's when you actually get good on the board. That's also when you get scarred up.

In 2 Samuel 16:5–13, there's this story about David getting out of Dodge. He didn't get too far before this guy named Shimei shows up and starts cursing David and throwing rocks and stuff at him. One of David's guys wants to go kill him, but David forbids him telling him not to worry about it. He said that Shimei might actually have been told by God to "Curse David." And David just owns it. He lets this dude follow him throwing curses, rocks, and dirt at him as he leaves home.

You know, we just don't ever see the big picture. Sometimes others have a vantage point that we don't. Our lives can be very self-centered, yet surprisingly un-self-aware. We totally judge others by their actions and give ourselves the grace to judge ourselves by our intention. But like Batman said, "It's not who I am underneath, but what I do that defines me." I feel like it's important to know how to take criticism that we don't always agree with, and be more aware of the environment we create around us. Like another quote I heard once from someone, "If one person calls you a jackass, just forget it. If 10 people call you a jackass, buy a saddle."

I would like to hope that I keep those two examples in mind in situations when I'm being verbally attacked. Both of these combined just speak to me of being true and honorable, as well as meek and humble. And not let anyone else have control of those parts of me, regardless of how they treat me.

Adam:
We all get misunderstood. You talk about not getting into defending yourself. What do you observe from the life of Jesus that informs how you move forward?

Benjamin:
The biggest thing that I caught about Jesus is how He faced His death day. People brought up accusations and stuff in front of the head honcho Pharisee dude, and Jesus never defended Himself. He was just silent about the accusations. For Jesus to defend Himself would be a way for Him to hide and escape His soon-coming fate. For Him to defend Himself would have been an act of bargaining for His life. But He didn't, He took a cold shower right there and embraced what was coming. He owned it! His life, His death, everything.

The other thing we talked about once, was how when Pilate asked Him what truth was, and He was silent. After our conversation that day, I interpreted that as Jesus communicating that truth isn't something that is simply told.

With that in mind, what do I observe from the life of Jesus that informs me on how to move forward? Defending yourself against people who are already hell-bent on killing you is a waste of time. No one was going to convince the other of anything that night anyway. Second, letting the truth about me be more than what I could explain with words to others, but let my actions and my heart define me to others. Just like we see with Batman... I mean Jesus.

Adam:
I know you've started blogging and I'm really excited about watching your progress. What else are you doing right now to push yourself towards living like the stuntman?

Benjamin:

Taking pride would be one thing. When I was a kid, I just had this innate understanding that I was less than. It was like everyone else's life was a television show that I knew was unrealistic, or at least unrealistic for me. I just watched life from the sidelines knowing I couldn't measure up. I'm not really sure where this idea/feeling/knowledge came from, but I had it. This all eventually evolved into me living a lifestyle that reflected my view of myself. Most of my life, I sent this message out, "I don't matter...." with the way I dressed and my appearance, how I ate, how I took care of myself, took care of my things, and let friends treat me. I was a mess, but I just accepted it as my role in life.

How I was living was incongruent with how Jesus saw me. He saw/sees me as valuable. I mean, you read the New Testament, and it tells you how much Jesus loves you. But that can still feel like watching the unreality television. But when I'd ask Him what He thought about me, personally, not just mankind, He'd say all of these great things. Greater things than I ever saw about me. None of it felt real, almost like Jesus was lying to me.

In the Bible (John 16), Jesus talks about how He's going to send the Holy Spirit, and how He's going to convict the world of sin, and the sin He mentions there, is the sin of not believing Jesus. So what do you do? View yourself as Jesus sees you, or sin by not believing Jesus, and think you're less than amazing because you don't feel that way?

So, to change how I think of myself, to line up with who He says I am, I have been adding pride to my life. Not that naughty sinful pride. I take better care of my vehicles now, I keep my home clean, and I take care of myself and my appearance, and expect to be treated better in relationships. Not to be arrogant or anything, but just to keep sending the message to myself that I'm valuable and not a "less than." It's about knowing my identity, not proving it.

For me this is a major "stuntman" issue. When the question is, "What? Do you really think you matter?" The cold shower response for me is, "Yes."

So let's sum this up: The grey man takes a warm shower, never lifts his head above the crowd, and doesn't try to skateboard or do any other sort of dangerous things. He eats his meals in front of a television, and most of all he avoids any opportunity to be real with other people. His dreams are subservient to his comfort, and so the dreams lose out. He's "comfortably numb" (as Pink Floyd would say). And he'll defend himself, because part of comfort is not letting people take stuff from you. The problem with grey man is that he's never more than a shadow of his real self; the self that would be in pursuit of dreams instead cowering from them.

The contrast is the stuntman who takes cold showers to jolt himself into action, dares to skateboard and risk pain, makes enemies not because he's mean but because he's real, allows people to curse him and doesn't defend his position, risks publishing things that might invite criticism, and more or less lives life in pursuit of excellence rather than in pursuit of comfort. Like Batman… I mean, more like Jesus, because he walks away from self-defense. The most telling thing about the trial you mentioned earlier is that Jesus answered him, "I have spoken openly to the world…. I always taught in synagogues or at the temple, where all the Jews come together. I said nothing in secret. Why do you question me? Ask those who heard me. Surely they know what I said."[74]

He said it all in public. He was no grey man.

Are excellence and comfort completely at odds with each other? I'm with you. I think you definitely can't pursue both at the same time. I've noticed that rock stars, celebrities, and others who pursue excellence for a time and become famous and rich often take comfort in that wealth and eventually the excellence they brought to the table can fade. Not always, but then they are the sorts of people about whom people say, "She's never content with what she did last year, she always wants more" because they know that the minute you begin to use your money to buy comfort, you're doomed.

❖ What can you do to become more of a stuntman and less of a grey man (or woman)?

Readers: I invite you to visit Benjamin Baker's blog at www.thebenjaminscott.com and leave him an encouraging comment.   *—Adam*

Final thoughts on Congo

I t is a rare moment in life when you get to go full circle this way. I stayed with Charles for 10 days at MPH Guesthouse in the western part of the city of Kinshasa. It was the same guesthouse our family stayed at in 1987 when we first arrived in Zaire. I was oriented to my surroundings immediately. The room was comfortable enough, breezy and in the low 70s at night, and because it was the end of the dry season, there weren't any mosquitos. The food was good; overall the accommodations were pleasant, which allowed us to focus on the training at hand.

One of our trainees, Jacques, asked me if I shouldn't be sleeping under a mosquito net. I said, "No, there aren't any mosquitoes right now, and besides, I feel good." "That's just the kind of fool they're looking for," he said. So I made sure to take preventative medicine against malaria.

We trained a group of 15 leaders in coaching. Charles led some extensive Bible study examining the ways in which the Leadership Coaching concept is not just a Western culture thing we were bringing to impose, showing the group how Barnabas used many of the same techniques and attitudes towards people to promote Paul.

When I led a piece of training on listening, I demonstrated the conversational technique of repeating what you've heard without adding your own interpretation or advice. Jacques said, "The village elders still know how to do this." It was exciting to see him contextualize the training on the fly, to recognize that there's at least one aspect that fits tightly with ancient cultural values—values the Kinois (residents of Kinshasa) are losing in the urban social landscape.

I was pleased to find that my French came back quickly and I was able to understand 90 percent or more of what the trainees were saying and deliver 75 percent of my training in French and 25 percent in English through our translator. Charles said that he was pleasantly surprised. It had been 10 years since I'd spent time in a francophone country (Senegal) and I expected to be rustier.

I gave credit to God first for that. Being able to converse in a common language is so helpful and being able to function felt like a miracle. I don't over-spiritualize it. I think there are several other reasons why this worked so well. First, I've been watching quite a few foreign/indie movies I can pick up at our public library, a lot of them in French with subtitles. Second, because of my childhood, the Kinois French accent is more familiar to my ear than other accents I've heard. Third, people were praying for me. That brings me full circle.

Any training like this requires follow-up, and it remains to be seen how the Congolese will manage to practice with each other. There are many challenges. It can cost at least $2 to get across town, an expense which may make face-to-face coaching prohibitive. Similarly, it is not unusual for Kinois to load their phone with $0.50 credit, and spending an hour on the phone with each other could also be prohibitive.

One evening at dinner, we talked with a reporter from NPR who was staying at the hostel overnight. He was investigating claims the World Bank made that we have little to worry about with the population exceeding seven billion, because, as he said, "They say that Congo alone can feed a billion." What was his take? "They need to feed their own people first!" And of course, the infrastructure is nowhere near where it would need to be to export food. In fact, much of the food consumed in Kinshasa is imported. You can get fresh food to the city from outlying areas within perhaps 30 miles. Beyond that, it becomes very challenging to get food to the city in a timely manner. And so the Kinois eat eggs from Brazil.

The point is, our trainees have economic hurdles we can't imagine if they want to continue practicing coaching. They can connect with the Internet, and I planned to coach one guy but when we began to use Skype, his connection was intermittent and we ended up conversing via Skype's chat function. It was a laborious process; difficult for me to say that I was really "coaching" but after all, at least he had an outside source with whom to share a challenging and personal problem. I was able to listen. Perhaps he walked away from that with some motivation!

Fears I had about the dangers of travel to one of the world's least stable nations were not completely unfounded. For myself, the worst that happened was some itchy fly bites around my ankles which persisted for at least a week after I got home.

But Kinshasa can be dangerous. Eight days after I left, Pastor Damien Kakhenda and his wife Sylvie were attacked by a street gang late at night. They were robbed, then the gang went after Damien with machetes, while he cried out, "Lord protect me!" until a gang member finally landed a blow to his head. They left him for dead. They chased Sylvie, who cried, "Why are you trying to kill us? You've already taken everything we have!" One gang member said, "Stop, stop!" but another hit her across the back with the flat side of an ax before they left.

Sylvie, fearing herself a widow, ran back to her husband, and said, "Pastor, get up, get up." He did; together they walked a kilometer to a clinic. There were concerns that Kakhenda whose head took a 10 centimeter gash, would need brain surgery, but the bleeding occurred outside the skull. The two are recuperating at the home of some missionaries as I write this. It appears that disaster had been averted, and friends rallied to send money to replace what was stolen and assist with medical bills. Disaster narrowly averted.

Why do we want to go back to Kinshasa to teach leadership skills to pastors? First, because people like Pastor and Mrs. Kakhenda exist. Damien was the trainee in this group who gave me a hard time, joked around and was generally fun to have in the group. In every group, there's one person like that who brings out the joy and sense of humor, plays off me in a way that helps me deliver my best. Humble-spirited, fun-loving, and gentle, Kakhenda is a

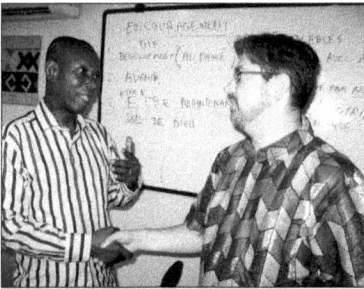

Figure 27. Pastor Damien Kakhenda gives the author encouragement.

true leader in Congo. But he is one of many, and he may be able to exemplify new paradigms for leadership for other leaders in the church. If the church can transform the way leadership is done, there's a possibility it could spread into the business and political realms as well.

Better leadership in the top echelons of the government would help the city of Kinshasa clean up the lawlessness that exists; and one day, we could hope a pastor and his wife could walk through the city without danger. The nation could learn to invest in infrastructure and could end up feeding us one day.

The vision and purpose for investing in leadership training for Congo (and Africa) has become personal. This is what happens when you meet people and listen to them. You will find they are worth investing in.

❖ Where do you have an opportunity to go back to your roots and give something to build a culture of listening and leadership?

It's me!
Lessons from Loctite

My favorite commercial from the Big Game 2015 was the Loctite glue spot, with very ordinary (read: not-Hollywood-beautiful) people singing and dancing about how Loctite saved their lives/marriages. The important words in this commercial, sung by an unknown actor, were, "It's me." (And the jingle continues: *If you make a thing or break a thing, it's no problem.*)

I found the "It's me" to be hilariously understated irony. Who is "me"? Everyman? Who is this guy? Then you realize it doesn't matter. It's a guy being himself, not to show off, not because he's a celebrity, but he's just there to celebrate the good life. "GLUE! LOCTITE, LOCTITE, YEAH."

The people in the ad were so genuinely abandoned to the party for this glue, so much that I wanted to get some of that glue too, I wanted it badly! Because it was funny and I LOVE funny. These guys were ME. They loved life, and they were goofy-looking and didn't care. That's me, too! I wanted to be part of them. I wanted some glue, my mouth was watering for it like I'd just seen a commercial for a cheeseburger. Not to eat the glue, but to be part of the crew.

I have this love/hate relationship with marketing myself. When I sabotage it, I end up with this thing where nobody wants to be part of the thing I'm doing. Which is sad, because this whole art of motivational listening thing is a great party. It's glue!

On the one hand, a false sense of humility pushes me away from doing a good job of building a personal brand—though if this book doesn't do it, I don't know what will. I don't want to be all about myself, I don't want to be the big-shot, or rather, though I have a temptation to want to become the big shot, like, being the star of *Oklahoma!*, I know I'm no Jon Bon Jovi. I'm more like the guy in the glue ad. I shy away from sharing all of myself with the world.

The process of writing this book has been gut-wrenching. It would be so much easier to hide behind characters in a novel. I worry about this: Do businessmen who want coaching care that I've written a novel? Do artists care about my work with missionaries enough to donate? Will my readers care what I think enough to engage some training? If they don't, will it be worth all the time I spent to write it? I have feet in so many worlds I feel more like a millipede than human, and a dancing one at that. But worrying about all these people and whether or not they care is immaterial. Maybe they don't, or won't, but they should. Because: GLUE!

Because I was afraid, I compartmentalized my worlds in an unhealthy way. That means for the past few years, I've scattered blog posts over six or eight different blog sites rather than having one blog that's just . . . me. I've hurt my readership by compartmentalizing my identity; and I hurt myself.

The other lesson from the ad was that the company itself went all in. I like that. I respect it. It's gutsy, risky, American to the core. They spent their entire ad budget for the YEAR on this 30-second spot: $4.5 MILLION. No compartmentalization. No little billboard over here for one type of industrial glue, no little magazine ad over there for a glue for home use. Just a hard core, one-shot branding exercise. I don't have stats, but I suspect it's working. Look: I'm still talking about it!

It's me, Adam G. Fleming. Not to impress you with my swanky middle initial, but to be known as a whole person, to be all in, to offer my unique perspective on motivation, art, and listening. Maybe you just want to read more, maybe you want to participate at some point. I will continue to write about this stuff, continue to train coaches, and to coach people.

So join my journey, it's a party for glue, because we just have to stick together! Subscribe to my blog and/ or my monthly e-newsletter for more material like what you've read here, at www.adamgfleming.com. Drop me a comment!

Acknowledgments

Pioneers, trainers and writers in the coaching world; Tony Stoltzfus, Lyn Eichmann, Doug Fike, Joseph Umidi, Paul Hillhouse, "P. S." in China, Jerry Park , Jerry Graham and many others.

Those who've believed in me enough to offer me opportunities to lead coach training workshops for their organizations: Tina Stoltzfus-Horst and Keisa Capers at CMI; Eldon Kibbey, Ralph Larimer, Paul Johnson and Kent Kussel at CBMC; Ron and Louise Burns; Jeff Williams; Charles Buller at AIMM. Without your support and promotion, I wouldn't have a career in this field today. The trainings I've led for you gave me income, improved my skills, sometimes resulted in paying clients, which kept me in coaching when I otherwise might have given up.

Support staff for training events; those who cook, organize meeting locations, transportation and so on. Invaluable stuff, and too often you go unnamed. Without Gary Yordy, Connie Adams, Carrie Jones and Maria Shisler, we really couldn't have done FOCOS in 2015 which was another major step forward for me.

Rich Foss, Tim Stair and the evolving board at Evergreen Leaders, and everyone who has donated to the non-profit work I do, including much of the work I do for the people and organizations in the second paragraph (above).

My three core communities, in no particular order, where people regularly step up to offer to wax my nose hairs: DSC guys who are waiting patiently for me to get back to works of fiction (you can hold me accountable to that) but who have mostly encouraged me to write, write, write, to hone my craft. Jonathan and Christa; Megan, *min Älskling*; Nate and Amber; Jason R.; and

Mark D. And members of the DSC crew who don't live in Goshen, too: It's your loss, but I guess not everyone can live here. Second, everyone at Thrive. Because we've proven you can disagree on theological points some would consider "major" and still love each other. That gives me courage to be edgy: I am sometimes wrong, but always loved. Finally, the heterogeneous, authentic, epic, meta-strangely attracted and deeply purposeful community of coaches at CMI retreats and training events, people from and working in more countries I can count. You guys expand my horizon continually, you help me question cultural issues and challenge me to be the best coach I can be.

Coaches I've had; it all started with Gary Horst; as well as two long-term peer coaches I've had, Geoff Graham and Mark Thomas, you practiced on me and trusted me to practice on you. You all listened to me ramble on. Somehow I ended up here.

My clients and trainees. You know who you are. Each one of you contributed to this book, too. You, more than anyone else, helped me hone my coaching style, and I have enjoyed working with every one of you.

My publisher and editor and others who read portions of the manuscript before it was done, trusting that I had something worth saying.

Dr. Mark Whitacre, thanks for the foreword. My colleagues in the appendix. Keep up the good work!

My blog readers, especially those who take a few extra moments to comment! My book readers, especially those who like what I have to say enough to buy multiple copies and pass them around. Thank you!

Other Listeners

The people and organizations listed in the following profiles are people I'm honored to call friends. It is a pleasure to introduce you to them. It is only fair to them to note a few things about their inclusion in this resource.

My writing does not necessarily reflect their thoughts or opinions on the subjects of a philosophy of listening, leadership or theology. There is a good chance that some of them will disagree with at least a few things I've said in the book. Their inclusion in the appendix should not be taken as a complete approval of whatever I say.

Some of them contributed to my Kickstarter project as I raised money to take the time to write the book, and the "Kickstarter reward" contained an agreement to include them. In other words, some of them did give me some money to support the writing of the book and in return I agreed to include them in this appendix. However, they all did so at my invitation: I would not have invited someone to participate in this appendix if I wasn't interested in promoting them in the first place, more to the point, I know they've had quality training in leadership coaching and can do a great job as your coach. Still others I decided to include as a gift.

I appreciate all of these people and hope that you will benefit from knowing who they are.

Karen Bontrager

Karen Bontrager's quest is to assist leaders and the teams and organizations they steward, in journeying well and reaching their highest contribution. While walking out this passion and through her own leadership story, she has cultivated a specialty.

Having a relationship with Karen gives strategic advantage to leaders who are navigating endings, beginnings and the crucial space between. Whether that space is transitional or sabbatical in nature, it massively impacts the following season and the ultimate contribution of the leader. Karen is known for the exhortation, "You win your next season in your transition/sabbatical." It is in this space where important processes can position a leader well for the next round. It is the difference between living and leading another season that is essentially the same, and a significantly elevated new season.

Karen's professional leadership coaching certification was acquired in 2006 and her coach training certification in 2007 through LifeForming Leadership Coaching. For close to a decade, Karen has utilized her gifts and training to serve individuals, teams, organizations and networks on four continents. As of September 2015, she had tallied over 2,500 hours of coaching and training.

The Midwest is home base for Karen, along with her husband of 30 years and two children in their twenties.

She may be contacted at karen.bontrager@gmail.com.

Jonathan Corbin

Jonathan lives in Goshen, Indiana with his wife, Anastasia, and four children.

Jonathan has had a life journey with a theme of helping people become aware of God's role in their everyday lives. His college degree launched him into church ministry from 2000–2005. He stepped away from this ministry in response to the desire to connect with individuals in a deeper way for life transformation.

In 2006, Jonathan developed a tree trimming business called My Tree Climber which he still runs as the owner-operator. He has gained valuable experience in a variety of small business ventures over the years. In 2010, Jonathan began meeting with a business and life transformation coach to refine his focus and efforts. He has worked with this coach now for five years, often in the capacity as a mentor coach. After a few years of intentional work, Jonathan clarified his passion for pursuing coaching as a personal calling.

Jonathan has been providing coaching services since 2013. He has a passion to help people discover purpose in their life and to make progress toward meaningful goals. Jonathan has participated in numerous short-term coach training events and is now working with Coaching Mission International to complete their Life Leadership Coach Training certification. He has a special interest in coaching business owners and entrepreneurs. He also specializes in nutrition and wellness coaching.

Contact information:
Jonathan E. Corbin
574-312-5072
Healthylife4u@solution4u.com

Doug Fike

Doug Fike lives in downtown Washington DC, where he moved with his wife, Charlene, following 20 years spearheading a coaching-based retreat center in Virginia's Allegheny Highlands.

Doug has been coaching since before it was a thing. In 1999, he convened a conclave for early practitioners which led to the formation of Transformational Leadership Coaching (later Lifeforming Leadership Coaching), of which he was a founding partner. Curriculum developed by Doug and his team has been widely translated and used around the world in the certification of over 1,000 coaches.

Over nearly three decades, thousands of alumni have been impacted by the Fikes' seminal "Life Focus" process. Coaches and organizations in various countries use the current version—Destiny Discovery Quest—to unleash and empower ordinary people to live extraordinary lives in all spheres of society.

Doug catalyzes a global leadership network through Growth Dynamics International, and convenes the virtual Life-Long Learning Community—connecting fellow travelers on a lifelong journey of transformation. Both of these feature coaching DNA at the core, and cultivate fresh coaching applications in an array of spheres and cultures. Feel free to check them out; both are open membership entities.

Transitions coaching is Doug's particular passion: organizational transitions, latter-stage life transitions, marriage/family transitions, sabbaticals at key junctures on the journey. He is currently exploring coach-based approaches to reconciliation and nation-building in war-torn central Africa. He serves as an executive coach for an array of business, church, NGO, and government leaders, and does some contract coaching in these areas. He can be contacted at doug@douglasfike.com.

Tina Stoltzfus Horst

Tina is the Executive Director of Coaching Mission International (CMI), a nonprofit organization dedicated to providing faith based, professional quality, cross-cultural coaching and coach training to missions' leaders.

Coaching Mission International's vision is that every missionary, grassroots national leader and mission organization staffer will have access to the support and individualized development that great coaching can offer! CMI has provided over 30,000 hours of coaching to missions in its 9-year history.

CMI provides coaching packages for individual missionaries and national leaders; and two missions coach training programs. FOCOS, Foundational Coach Training, is a one-year program including coaching, mentor coaching, onsite training and teleclasses to enable missions' leaders to integrate coaching skills into their ministry. Mission Coach Training (MCT), includes training in life purpose coaching, and the most thorough training on cross-cultural missions coaching available; with graduates completing the 2-year program with 200 hours of coaching experience. For more information on CMI's vision and programs, go to: www.cmiprograms.org. CMI contracts with 25 coaches and coach trainers from around the world.

Tina was trained by LifeForming Leadership Coaching over a decade ago and has over 2,000 hours of coaching and training experience. She is a member of Christian Coaches Network. She loves to coach leaders and has particular expertise and interest in cross-cultural issues, women in leadership, and of course, missions coaching! She lives in Goshen, Indiana, with her husband Gary (also a coach), and is the mother of two adult children, Ben and Rosie. She relaxes in the garden with her dog, Fia, or with a good book.

You can reach Tina at director@cmiprograms.com.

Michael Pollock

Michael V. Pollock currently lives in Muskegon, Michigan with his wife, Kristen, and youngest daughter, Anna.

Michael began coaching in China after experiencing the power of coaching for himself. He completed his training in 2012 through Creative Results Management including 100 hours of coaching and training. An educator by training with over 20 years' experience in classrooms and administration, Michael loves the "aha" moments of discovery and transformation. He founded Daraja in 2012 to provide resources and training to cross-cultural young adults.

An adult Third Culture Kid and son of missionaries himself and the father of 3 TCKs, Michael focuses on coaching young adult TCKs in their late teens and twenties as they transition into adult life, often cross-culturally. He has logged over 120 hours with young adult TCKs on multiple continents and taught a CEU seminar for CMI, Coaching Missions International.

Along with individual coaching, Michael is available to teach seminars on TCK care and transition. He sees coaching, along with mentoring, as powerful tools providing care and cultivation for a flourishing life. Constantly teaching and learning, he welcomes invitations from organizations, universities and churches to speak and present.

Michael can be contacted at mvp.at.work@gmail.com and his work at Daraja is online at www.daraja.us.

Mark & Laurie Thomas

Mark and Laurie have been married for 35 years and live in Castle Rock, Colorado where they have invested the last 20 years serving their Lord Jesus Christ as church leaders and business owners. They are blessed with four children and a son-in-law, all of whom live close to them.

Mark and Laurie are both Board Certified Biblical Counselors and certified Prepare/Enrich facilitators. They began relationship coaching in 2011 having been trained as Marriage Coaches by Great Relationships. Relationship coaching allows them to act on their passion to encourage and empower couples to grow ever closer in their relationship with the Lord Jesus Christ and each other. The couples that have received coaching from them have made a proactive decision to have a great relationship, not settling for just a good relationship. Mark and Laurie are impacting marriages with "To Know & Be Known, A Marriage Workshop" which is provided in a live day-long interaction and an online training. These workshops along with the personal coaching provided, empower couples with the heart, hope and skill to grow and go on with each other in a sustainable fashion to fulfill their calling that the Lord Jesus Christ has revealed to them. These couples continue to grow ever closer in their relationship and ultimately achieve their goal of finishing strong.

Along with couples coaching, Mark is also a professional Cross Cultural Life & Leadership Coach and Coach Trainer. He has been trained by PCCI (Professional Christian Coaching Institute) and CMI (Coaching Missions International). He has provided over 750 hours of coaching to couples, missionaries, pastors, ministry leaders and business clients.

Their web presence is PathLight.pro where you are invited to contact Mark or Laurie at Mark-Laurie@PathLight.pro, or call Mark at 720-272-7466.

Jerimae Yoder

Jerimae Yoder is the Director of Coaching at Worship Team Coach.com. He has been coaching since 2011 but recently found his niche as a coach for worship leaders and musicians. Worship Team Coach has trained thousands of worship leaders through online videos, blogs and workshops and is now using traditional coaching methods to help leaders catapult to the next level of leadership. Jerimae's true passion and burden is to see musicians become amazing leaders in the church and in the music industry.

Jerimae resides in Norwalk, Ohio, is married to Karen and has four amazing children. He has been a worship leader since 1997 as a volunteer, part-time and full-time staff. He has been a national recording artist and toured extensively. Jerimae also is a coach/mentor for the Objective movement and the Extreme tour.

Connect with Jerimae at
Jerimae@worshipteamcoach.com
Online at www. worshipteamcoach.com

Glossary

Buoyancy: faith-based tolerance for risk. Motivational listeners invite people to test it.

Candidate for a Wax Job: 1) anyone who needs their nose hairs regularly waxed, 2) those who need outside perspective, 3) everyone.

Edge of the world: place where our perception changes, the wind is visible, where the mundane meets the extraordinary, where breakthrough can happen, where the limited/contained meets the unlimited/uncontained, where conditions for risk taking are presented.

Expanding truth: the truth, plus any potential truths that could be; the expansion upon it made possible by the imagination and knowable in the gut.

Fact: a thing or event that has happened at a point in time which may or may not be superfluous to truth.

Fiction: any imagined world which gives us a glimpse of expanded truth.

George Gobel: (n) 1) an evasive tall tale which tells you nothing, 2) an intentional deflection of direct response to a speaker's request for the listener's opinion or knowledge; with intent to provoke the speaker's own curiosity or ability to come to their own conclusions. (Vt 1) to recognize the fact that your opinion is irrelevant, further, to disguise whether or not you know or have an answer.

Good guy: a particularly personal green duck which involves a belief in one's own inherent goodness, a lack of sonder and a position which promotes self-defense.

Green duck: lack of awareness of one's own fixed assumptions and worldview which limit possibilities. Unexamined fundamentalism. Painted Black Swan event.

Grey man/stuntman: the grey man escapes for the sake of comfort, the stuntman takes the cold shower and embraces criticism.

Hedgerows: hedgerows are a semi-wild place for child-like exploration, and the growth of uncultivated things: a place where foxes live, where mushrooms and blackberries grow. A space broader than your margins or Sabbath day. A place to wander and wonder on your way to the *edge of the world*.

Jesus in Jeopardy: the cultural impact of multiple green ducks.

Memory: a fact covered with the patina and grime of time from which we can draw principles.

Middle of nowhere: A place of under-connection *OR Over-connection* (like the Internet) where we lose touch with surface tension and face potential to drown/ get lost.

Mobilized kingdom proletariat: Common, defenseless, unknown workers actively bearing children.

Painting your duck green: intentionally limiting or forcing conformity based on prior fixed assumptions in spite of evidence. Choosing fundamentalism.

Risk: an opportunity to choose an action or to not act, 2) the more challenging of two options.

Self-defense: the act of closing yourself off to possibilities which may hurt you, 2) limiting damage.

Sonder: the recognition that others have a complex story [not my own term].

Sourdough motivation culture: a place where individual and corporate purpose, harmony and change, and outside perspective all work together.

Surface tension: the heightened awareness felt at the edge of the known world, where decisions of risk happen and a clear picture of our own buoyancy is essential.

Truth: as accurate an account of reality as is made possible by gathering facts together.

Vortex Street: the consistent eddies created by a permanent obstacle, 2) the drag from those eddies which add to our challenges.

Illustrations

Notes

1 . Kurt Vonnegut, *Slapstick or Lonesome No More!: A Novel* (New York: Dial Press Trade an imprint of Random House, 1976).
2. John 8:32b.
3. Nassim Nicholas Taleb, *The Black Swan: The Impact of the Highly Improbable* (New York: Random House, 2008), xxii–xxiii.
4. Wikipedia article on Eephus Pitch.
5. Wikipedia article.
6. Webster's New World Dictionary, 3rd College Ed., [emphasis added].
7. Wendell Berry, "The Loss of the University" *Home Economics* (New York: North Point Press, 1987).
8. 2 Samuel 12:13a.
9. Luke 15:11–32.
10. Matthew 18:3–5.
11. Ibid.
12. 2 Samuel 12:1–4.
13. John 14:6a.
14. Matthew 7:14.
15. Acts 10:34b, King James Version.
16. Raymond A. Mar, Keith Oatley, Jacob Hirsh, Jennifer dela Paz, Jordan B. Peterson, "Bookworms versus nerds: Exposure to fiction versus non-fiction, divergent associations with social ability, and the simulation of fictional social worlds," *Journal of Research in Personality* (Toronto, Ontario, Canada: University of Toronto, September 15, 2005).
17. Ecclesiastes 1:9b, 2:17b.
18. Laura Beil, "The Certainty of Memory Has Its Day in Court," *New York Times*, November 28, 2011.
19. Public Broadcasting Service.
20. Henry David Thoreau, *Walden; or Life in the Woods and Civil Disobedience* (New York: Harper Classics, 1958, 1965), 69–70.
21. Ibid., 71.
22. Radley Balko, "A Brief History of Forensics," *Washington Post*, April 21, 2015.
23. David Comer Kidd and Emanuele Castano, "Reading Literary Fiction Improves Theory of Mind," *Sciencexpress Report*, The New School for Social Research, New York, October 3, 2013.
24. Eva Maria Koopman and Frank Hakemulder, "Effects of Literature on Empathy and Self-Reflection: A Theoretical-Empirical

Framework" *De Gruyter*, JLT 2105; 9(1): 79–111, 87, quoting Keith Oatley, *General Psychology*, vol. 3(2), June 1999, 101–117.

25. Ibid., 88.
26. Ibid.
27. Nassim Nicholas Taleb, *Bed of Procrustes: Philosophical and Practical Aphorisms* (New York: Random House, 2010).
28. Ibid.
29. Robert Kunzig, *National Geographic*, "The Will to Change" November, 2015, 32–63.
30. Luke 18:19.
31. YouTube video transcript by Adam Fleming. https://www.youtube.com/watch?v=_8rbHwMXMT8.
32. http://www.mlive.com/news/grand-rapids/index.ssf/2013/09/mother_who_witnessed_fatal_sho.html.
33. http://www.mlive.com/news/grand-rapids/index.ssf/2013/11/morning_review_video_shows_dri.html.
34. Luke 10:25–37.
35. John 18:38a.
36. John 18:1–14.
37. John Koenig, *The Dictionary of Obscure Sorrows*, www.dictionaryofobscuresorrows.com.
38. http://www.huffingtonpost.com/2012/06/03/religious-pilgrimages-spiritual-_n_1564664.html.
39. Matthew 25:36.
40. Luke 4:24.
41. James 3:1.
42. National Public Radio.
43. National Basketball Association.
44. A U.S. based global cable and satellite television channel.
45. Mark Twain, *The Adventures of Huckleberry Finn* (United Kingdom: Watermill Press, 1988), 358.
46. Ibid., 360.
47. http://www.goodreads.com/quotes/28017-i-m-not-a-very-good-writer-but-i-m-an-excellent.
48. https://www.flickr.com/photos/pazzani/4341808005/. Mike's Birds, February 6, 2010. Converted to black and white.
49. Genesis 1:3, 14.
50. Romans 8:19 (J. B. Phillips' translation).
51. Taleb, *Bed of Procrustes.*
52. Umberto Eco, translated by William Weaver, *Postscript to the Name of The Rose* (San Diego: Harcourt Brace Jovanovich, 1984).

53. Donald Miller, *Blue Like Jazz: Nonreligious Thoughts on Christian Spirituality* (Nashville: Thomas Nelson, 2003).

54. *Science Friday*, May 3, 2013.

55. Michael Pollan, *Cooked: A Natural History of Transformation* (New York: Penguin Books, 2014).

56. Robert M. Pirsig. *Zen and the Art of Motorcycle Maintenance: An Inquiry into Values* (New York: William Morrow and Co., 1974).

57. Daniel H. Pink, *Drive: The Surprising Truth about What Motivates Us* (New York: Riverhead Books, 1995).

58. Jeffrey Tayler, *Facing the Congo: A Modern-Day Journey into the Heart of Darkness* (New York: Three Rivers Press, 2000).

59. Tony Stoltzfus, *Leadership Coaching: The Disciplines, Skills and Heart of a Christian Coach* (Virginia Beach, VA: Tony Stoltzfus, 2005), 16.

60. Scott Meslow, *The Atlantic*, May 24, 2012 http://www.theatlantic.com/entertainment/archive/2012/05/a-brief-history-of-time-travel-in-movies/257638/.

61. John Donne, *Devotions Upon Emergent Occasions*, Meditation 17, 1624.

62. Mark 14:7a.

63. Jonathan Reuel, Watershed, "Better Days."

64. Photo by Clyde Robinson, September 15, 2009. https://www.flickr.com/photos/crobj/3923226306. Converted to black and white.

65. Wendell Berry, "Getting Along with Nature," *Home Economics* (New York: North Point Press, 1987), 13.

66. Barbara Kingsolver, *Flight Behavior: A Novel* (New York: Harper-Collins, 2012).

67. Nancy Sleeth, "The Most Ignored Commandment" http://www.relevantmagazine.com/god/practical-faith/most-ignored-commandment.

68. Taleb, *Bed of Procrustes*.

69. David Van Reybrouck, *Congo: The Epic History of A People;* translated from the Dutch by Sam Garrett (New York: Ecco, an imprint of HarperCollins, 2014), 440.

70. Pink, *Drive*.

71. John 18:38b.

72. John 13:21–30.

73. 2 Peter 3:9b.

74. John 18:20–21.

About the Author
Adam G. Fleming

Adam G. Fleming lives in Goshen, Indiana, with his family. His children inspire him most often by popping into his home office while he's writing to ask life's most urgent and relevant question: "Where's Mom?"

He's a normal family man during the evening hours, but at dawn he puts on his mask, tights and cape and goes to work as the CEO of Evergreen Leaders, partnering with several organizations to provide coaching for leaders and training more coaches to multiply *motivational listening* internationally. Adam has provided over 1,000 hours of coaching and training since 2009 and his past and current clients and trainees work in dozens of countries.

He also coaches writers; as well as nonprofit leaders who raise their own support with Evergreen Leaders' unique fundraising system *Greenlight Fundraising* (an Entrust Source book by Rich Foss). He is a member coach of Christian Coaches Network International.

The author's hobbies include vintage base ball, Scrabble, reading, picking berries along hedgerows, watching French movies and taking long romantic walks on the beach. He has so many hobbies it's a wonder he ever finishes books, but he does: Adam's first novel, *White Buffalo Gold,* was published in 2012. For more great content:

Follow Adam's blog: www.adamgfleming.com
Subscribe to his monthly newsletter: adamgfleming.com/news
email any comments/questions:
adam.fleming.lifecoach@gmail.com

Note: If you'd like to know more about Adam's nonprofit work or to join his team through your financial support, you can visit evergreenleaders.org.

www.ingramcontent.com/pod-product-compliance
Lightning Source LLC
Chambersburg PA
CBHW071333210326
41597CB00015B/1438